Other Running Press Glossaries

Real Estate Language
Sailing Language
Computer Terms
Banking Language
Astrology Terms

Running Press Glossary
of

Baseball
Language

Richard Scholl

Running Press
Philadelphia, Pennsylvania

Copyright © 1977 Running Press

All rights reserved under the Pan-American and
    International Copyright Conventions

Distributed in Canada by Van Nostrand Reinhold, Ltd.,
    Ontario, Canada

International Representatives: Kaimon & Polon, Inc.,
    456 Sylvan Avenue, Englewood Cliffs, New Jersey 07632

Printed in the United States of America

1 2 3 4 5 6 7 8 9

First digit on left indicates the number of this printing.

Library of Congress Cataloging in Publication Data

Scholl, Richard, 1953–
    Running Press Glossary of Baseball Language
    Summary: A glossary with more than 800 entries of terminology
and jargon used in baseball.
    1. Baseball—Dictionaries. [1. Baseball—Dictionaries] I. Title.
II. Title: Glossary of baseball language.
GV867.3.S36   796.357'03   77-410
ISBN 0-914294-79-2 Library binding
ISBN 0-914294-80-6 Paperback

Series editor and designer: Peter J. Dorman
Cover design: Jim Wilson
Cover illustration: Laurie Marks
Interior illustration: Linda Grossman

Cover printed by Harrison Color Process Lithographers, Willow
    Grove, Pennsylvania
Typography: Century Textbook, by Comp•Art, Philadelphia,
    Pennsylvania
Printed and bound by Port City Press, Baltimore, Maryland

This book may be ordered directly from the publisher.
Please include 25ᵉ postage.

Try your bookstore first.

Running Press
38 South Nineteenth Street
Philadelphia, Pennsylvania 19103

Preface

Almost every profession and occupation that we can think of has a specialized vocabulary of its own, and baseball is certainly no exception. Baseball relies on a unique terminology that allows players, coaches, announcers, and fans to understand each other. Terms and expressions arise because enthusiasts must be able to discriminate among highly specific meanings of a general vocabulary if they are to communicate quickly and efficiently. When a baseball coach instructs a runner to "steal," he does not have to tell him "Advance to the next base as soon as the pitcher begins to throw toward the plate." The meaning is conveyed in a language that has been adapted to a very particular need.

Without their vocabulary, baseball buffs would be doomed to wordiness to express even the simplest concept. But for those who did not grow up frequenting neighborhood "sandlots," little league "diamonds," or big league stadiums, a baseball announcer's lingo may sound more like Greek than English. Unfamiliarity with the language of baseball may prevent a fan who has developed a sudden interest in the action from enjoying the game—particularly a female, who has had less exposure to our national sport.

For the uninformed spectator, a baseball glossary is a valuable tool. And fans who know the game well will continue to be surprised at the scope and subtleties of the baseball language. About one-third of this book is concerned with fundamental definitions. The remainder explores slang expressions heard on and off the field, and situations and rules that arise only seldomly.

—Richard Scholl

Abbreviations. (1) *Batting.* **AB:** official at bats. **BB:** walks. **CS:** caught stealing. **G:** games. **H:** hits. **HR:** home runs. **R:** runs. **RBI:** runs batted in. **S:** sacrifices. **SF:** sacrifice fly. **SB:** stolen bases. **SO:** strikeouts. **2b:** doubles. **3b:** triples.

(2) *Fielding.* **A:** assists. **DP:** double plays. **E:** errors. **PO:** putouts. **TR:** triple play.

(3) *Pitching.* **CG:** complete games. **ER:** earned runs. **ERA:** earned run average. **GS:** games started. **H:** hits allowed. **HB:** hit batters. **IP:** innings pitched. **K:** strikeouts. **R:** runs allowed. **SO:** strikeouts. **SHO:** shutouts. **WP:** wild pitches.

Aboard. On base; to occupy a base.

Ace. A team's most effective and reliable pitcher.

Across body. When a fielder *backhands* the ball, he usually throws with his arm extended across his chest and very close to his opposite shoulder, rather than straight ahead away from his body.

Activate. To return a player to the active *roster* after he has been out of action because of injury, disablement, or suspension.

Advance. To move safely from one base to another on a hit, sacrifice, or steal. A runner on second is in a position to advance home on a *hit* to the outfield.

Aggressive hitter. One who steps very confidently toward the pitcher; often he will swing at any pitch that is even close to the strike zone.

Ahead of the count. When the batter at the plate has fewer *strikes* on him than *balls*. If the *count* on the batter is 3 and 1, for example, he is said to be ahead of the count.

Aiming. Describes a pitcher straining to throw a strike and disturbing his natural motion.

Alibi. An excuse made for poor hitting, fielding, pitching or coaching; or for absence from a game or practice.

All runners breaking. With two outs and a count of 3 balls and 2 strikes on the batter, all runners begin to advance (i.e., break) toward the next base while the pitcher is winding up. Because the batter must either strike out, walk, hit a foul ball, be put out, or get a hit, the runner(s) takes no risk in trying to advance.

All Star Game. Annually on a day in July the best players from the National *League* meet the best from the American. Fans select the first string by a balloting process, and the manager picks the second string, the pitching staff, and the coaches. At least one representative must be chosen from every team in both Major Leagues.

All-American. A college or high school player voted one of the most outstanding baseball players in the country, a distinction which increases his chances of being signed by the pros.

Alley. (1) The heart of the plate. See also *Down the pipe.* (2) The gap in either right-center or left-center field.

Alligator mouth. A player who boasts or derides other players but lacks the courage to back up his words.

All-time. Those active players and old-timers considered the best in baseball history.

Amateur. A player who is not professional. He may belong to one of many leagues established for players between the ages of 8 and 25, including Little League, Babe Ruth, Pony, Colt, and the American Junior League.

American League. See *League.*

Appeal. Describes a situation in a game that is subject to re-evaluation. (1) A fielder claims to the umpire that the offensive team has violated the rules because a runner fails to tag up or touch a base. (2) A batter or the catcher asks the home plate umpire to consult either the first or third base umpire for a ruling on a swing; or the umpire makes the request independently. (3) See also *Protest*.

Apple. A common term for a baseball.

Arbiter. An umpire. There may be from 1 to 6 men in blue to rule over a game, depending on how many umps a particular league can afford or a specific game warrants. For example, amateur leagues often employ 1 umpire for first and second base and another for third and home. In playoffs, World Series, and All Star games in the majors, 6 umpires generally take the field.

Around the horn. An expression which describes the action of throwing the ball around the infield for practice; or, during the game, the ball is thrown around the horn after the first or second out is made, only if none of the bases are occupied.

Art. Refers to the intuitive and instinctual ability of a player or coach to respond adeptly to a game situation.

Artificial turf. Synthetic field surface which resembles grass in color and appearance; designed for resiliency and durability. Astroturf, which receives its name from Houston's Astrodome (where it was installed), is one of the earliest and most popular of synthetic grasses.

Assist. Any deflection or throw of the ball by one fielder to another fielder contributing to a *put-out*.

Astroturf. See *Artificial turf*

At-bat. An official appearance at the plate. An at-bat is recorded unless the batter walks, sacrifices, is interfered with by the catcher, or is hit by a pitch. The official at-bat is one statistic used in determining a hitter's *average*.

Athletic hose. Thin, high white socks worn under colored stockings to prevent blood poisoning in the event that a player gets *spiked.*

Athletic supporter. Elastic piece of equipment worn under the player's uniform around the waist for protection of the groin.

Autographed ball. A souvenir baseball signed by any number of players on one or more teams.

Average. (1) Batting: Number of official times *at-bat* divided by the number of *hits,* to the nearest thousandth. For example, a batter with 3 hits in 9 times at bat averages .333. At-bats do not include walks, sacrifices, hit-by-pitch, or catcher's interference. (2) Fielding: Number of *put-outs* divided by number of fieldable plays. For example, a fielder with 1 error in 10 plays averages .900. (3) Pitching: See *Earned run average.*

Away game. A game played on another team's field; the team that has to travel is the visiting team. In the Major Leagues each club plays half of its 162 games away.

Back-door slide. Performed when the runner sees that he will be beaten by the throw. In desperation, he feigns a *hook slide* but goes beyond the base, reaching back with his hand, hoping to confuse the fielder.

Backhand. When the ball is hit to the side opposite that of the fielder's glove, he must reach across his body and turn his wrist backwards to catch the ball. This is a backhand maneuver.

Backing up. (1) Throw: A player backs up a fellow fielder when he positions himself at some distance behind that fielder who is receiving the throw. (2) Hit: A fielder runs behind another fielder who is pursuing a hit ball in case the ball gets through.

Backstop. Either the permanent fence or wire cage surrounding the batting area on an amateur field, or the net that protects fans from foul balls behind home plate in Major League stadiums.

Bad-ball hitter. A batter who is better at hitting pitches that are out of the *strike zone* than pitches that are well within the strike zone. For this kind of hitter to be consistent is a rarity.

Bad hop. A bounding ball which suddenly changes course by veering upward or to one side when the ball hits a stone or other object on the field.

Bag. Term for *base;* in particular, first, second, or third base.

Baiting the hitter. When the pitcher throws the ball just beyond the strike zone, usually *outside,* to try to get the batter to swing at a bad pitch, he is said to be baiting the hitter.

Bailing out. Describes a batter who is fooled by a pitch, strides too soon, and takes his eye off the ball; or is afraid of the fastball and steps toward third base.

Balk. An unnatural or unorthodox movement made by the pitcher in his *delivery* to the plate. For example, pitching from the stretch without first coming to a set position; faking a throw to home or to another base with his foot on the rubber; pitching when the catcher is out of his box; or pumping more than twice during a warmup. If no runners are on base, the balking move is counted as a *ball;* if there is one or more runner aboard, each advances one base when the umpire calls the balk.

Ball. (1) Any pitch outside the *strike zone* not swung at by the batter. Four balls constitute a *walk,* by which the batter is awarded a free trip to first base. (2) See *Baseball (2).*

Ball boy (*or* **girl).** Someone who chases foul balls and keeps them off the field surface to prevent injuries; also supplies the umpire with fresh baseballs as needed throughout the course of a game.

Ballpark. A team's field or stadium.

Baltimore chop. A batted ball that bounces only once or twice very high off the ground. It is usually easy to field, although the runner has a good chance of beating it out.

Bare-handed. Fielders sometimes have to catch the ball in this manner—without using the glove—especially on bunts and slow rollers where they may have to make a quick, off-balanced throw.

Base. Each of the four corners of the *diamond.* Except for home plate, each base is a white canvas bag filled with stuffing, 15 inches square and 3 to 4 inches high, tied with straps to metal stakes. Only one runner may occupy a base at any one time. In the majors, they are 90 feet apart; 60 to 75 feet apart for amateurs; and 60 feet for softball.

Base hit. Usually refers to a *single,* but may actually be any hit. A double, for example, is called a two-base hit. See also *Hit.*

Base lines. Chalk lines connecting home plate and first, and home and third; and imaginary lines connecting first and second, and second and third. The four lines joined together form a *diamond.* A runner may deviate from these lines by 3 feet to either side unless he is avoiding interference with a fielder or is rounding a base, in which case he is permitted to deviate by 15 feet.

Base on balls. A *walk.*

Base paths. The 6-foot wide lanes, centered by the *base lines,* in which the runner is permitted to travel.

Base sticker. A runner who takes either a very short *lead* or none at all.

Baseball. (1) Familiarly known as our national sport, a game involving 18 participants, 9 on each side. The team on defense employs a pitcher, catcher, 4 infielders, and 3 outfielders. The team on offense is comprised of the batters who come to the plate to hit, run, and score. Behind the catcher is the umpire, or arbiter, who enforces the rules, calls balls and strikes, makes calls at the plate, etc. Offensive and defensive play alternates. A team remains offensive—at bat—until 3 outs are made against it; then it goes to the defense—on the field—and stays there until the opposition incurs 3 outs. One such cycle of batting and fielding constitutes one inning. The object of the game is to score more runs—have more batters come around safely to home plate—than the opposition within 9 innings of play. A tie score at the end of this period sends the game into extra innings, which continue until one team breaks the tie. The home team always has the last opportunity at bat.

(2) A white horsehide sphere weighing 5 to $5\frac{3}{4}$ ounces and measuring 9 to $9\frac{3}{4}$ inches around. The baseball comprises an internal core of cork and rubber wrapped in many layers of yarn. Its outer cover is tightly stitched, stretched leather.

Baseball Annie. A girl or young woman who likes being seen with a professional player. The meaning of this term has changed somewhat in recent years to encompass the whole colorful array of fans who enjoy frequenting spring training camps.

Baseball cards. Collected mostly by young boys, they contain the player's picture and data concerning his position, physical attributes, and career performance.

Baseball toss. A competition where players see who can throw the ball the farthest; accuracy is also taken into account.

Base-running. The art of maneuvering on the base paths, including techniques of stealing, breaking up double plays, getting a good lead or a quick jump, the hit-and-run, the bunt-and-run, sliding, and scoring.

Basket catch. A style of catching in which the fielder cups his hands against his body, usually at the waist, to haul in a fly ball (usually a high fly or a pop-up).

Bat. A wooden or aluminum stick, smooth and rounded, measuring at most 2 ¾ inches in diameter at its thickest or meatiest part, and extending a maximum of 42 inches in length. Bats are now most commonly made from ash; formerly, they were commonly made of willow.

Bat boy. The youth who arranges the equipment in its place before and during a game. He retrieves the bat after it is dropped by the hitter.

Bat grip. The rubber or synthetic coating on the knob and handle of a bat, designed for better grip and to prevent chipping of the wood.

Bat weight. A circular ring of heavy metal that slides on any bat to serve the same purpose as the *lead bat,* namely strengthening the arms so that the bat feels lighter at the plate.

Batter. The hitter at the plate who tries to get on base via a *walk* or *hit.* He may also arrive safely on base as a result of a fielder's error, or by being struck by a pitched ball. He is *out* if he strikes out and the catcher holds onto the ball; if he hits a fly or a line drive caught by a fielder; if he hits a grounder and the ball is thrown to first base before he reaches that base; or if he is tagged out by a fielder with the ball while running toward any base.

Batter's boxes. Two rectangular sections measuring 4 feet by 6 feet on either side of the plate. The batter must remain in this area until the pitcher delivers the ball. (See p. 93.)

Batter's cage. A portable backstop constructed of metal or wire mesh; used for batting practice.

Batter's glove. A thin leather or vinyl garmet resembling a golf glove; worn by a hitter for better grip and for support of the hand muscles.

Battery. The pitcher-catcher combination in the lineup for either team.

Batting around. Occurs whenever any hitter bats twice within one inning without violating the batting order.

Batting defensively. Describes a situation when a hitter has 2 strikes on him, or is batting in a crucial situation. As a defensive strategy, his priority may be to hit the ball at any cost rather than to hit as hard as he can.

Batting order. The sequence in which a team's players will bat. This lineup must be presented to the umpire prior to the start of a game.

Batting out of turn. A batter is out when he violates the order presented to the umpire on the lineup card at the game's outset. As soon as he takes a swing, the batter out-of-turn is called out by the umpire.

Batting streak. Applies to a player who has hit safely (gotten at least one hit) in consecutive games. A long streak is a very difficult feat, especially in the Major Leagues.

Batting title. The honor accorded the player in each league with the highest *average* by the season's end; in the majors, a player must bat a minimum of 502 times to be eligible.

Beanball. An illegal pitch thrown intentionally at a batter's head, possibly resulting in the pitcher's being ejected from the game.

Beat out. When a ball is hit to an infielder and the batter reaches first before the throw and without an error being committed, he is said to have beat it out, and is awarded a *hit*.

Beating the throw. Refers to a runner's reaching a base safely before the ball arrives.

Behind the count. Refers to a batter who has more strikes against him than balls. For example, a batter with one ball and two strikes is behind the count.

Behind the runner. Since a runner's direction is counterclockwise, a batter will often try to hit to right field, or opposite the direction in which the runner is headed. This is known as hitting behind the runner.

Bench. (1) Long seat in the dugout for players and coaches. (2) Refers, collectively, to the players who are not starters.

Bent-leg slide. A normal slide, usually straight into the base, where the runner bends one leg at about a 45-degree angle.

Best interest clause. The commissioner's legal sanction to take action when he thinks that the dignity and professional demeanor of baseball might be threatened by a club's activities.

Big bill. The final bounce into a fielder's glove on a high bounding grounder; so-called because of the ease of the catch.

Bird dogs. Friends or associates of a *scout* who keep him informed of budding prospects for the Major Leagues.

Blank. To hold a team scoreless.

Blaster. A player who is notorious for frequently voicing his opinions of the team or the management to the club's administration.

Bleachers. Inexpensively priced seats, usually wooden benches, situated just beyond or at the far corners of the outfield.

Bleeder. A slow roller that barely eludes a fielder; or a bad hop that bounces beyond a fielder's reach, resulting in a *hit*.

Blocking the plate. When a runner is advancing toward the plate and the catcher receives a throw, the catcher may use his body to prevent the runner from touching home while tagging the runner out.

Bloop. A weakly hit fly ball into the infield or shallow outfield that is very difficult for a fielder to get to; usually results in a *hit*.

Blow up. Refers to a pitcher who becomes unglued rather suddenly and either loses his *control* or begins to give up many hits.

Blue darter. A hard *line drive.*

Bobble. To juggle or drop the ball.

Boiler. A player's stomach, particularly when it is upset by pre-game nervousness.

Bolt. A blemish, usually a pimple or a boil. When a player gets a "wrench on that bolt," he is finding a way of getting rid of it.

Boner. A derogatory term which refers to a fielding *error.*

Bonus baby. An expression which refers to an amateur player who signs a professional contract at a figure above the minimum allowed by the league because of his exceptional ability.

Book. (1) The official rules. (2) Tablet of scorecards. (3) Generally recognized guidelines for strategy. (4) The pitcher's or batter's knowledge of the other's strengths and weaknesses.

Bookends. Back-to-back games with identical scores recorded by a team or pitcher.

Boot. A muff or error.

Bottle bat. A bat which has a concave surface at its very top, resulting in reduced air friction on the swing.

Bottom. (1) Of *inning:* The time when the home team bats, consisting of 3 put-outs. If the home team is ahead after the visitors have batted in the ninth inning, only half of an inning is played. (2) Of the *order:* The last few hitters in the lineup, down to the pitcher, who usually bats last.

Bounder. A high-bouncing ground ball usually fielded without too much difficulty.

Box score. The published record of a game, including data on the hitters' and pitchers' performances, errors committed, extra base hits, number of men left on base, and strikeouts.

Break. (1) Good or bad twist of luck. (2) Deviation in the trajectory of a pitch. (3) A runner's advance toward the next base during the pitcher's delivery.

Breaking ball. Any pitch that fluctuates noticeably from its natural trajectory, such as the *curve, slider, drop, screwball,* or *knuckler.*

Break-up slide. When the possibility of a double or triple play exists, the runner slides into the fielder who is making a relay. This action on the part of the runner forces the fielder off balance, thereby hampering a good throw.

Bring in. To hit or *sacrifice* a runner to the plate for a score.

Broken bat. Cracks or splintering usually occur when the pitch strikes the handle or when the ball hits parallel with the grain of the wood rather than perpendicular to it.

Broken wrist. Not the injury, but the batter's rolling his wrists as he swings. If he begins his swing and then stops suddenly without turning the wrists, it is a *check swing.*

Brush. The small whisk or wire-bristle brush used by the umpire for dusting off home plate.

Brush-back. A pitch thrown inside to intimidate the batter.

"Bug on the rug." An expression referring to a grounder which eludes one or more fielders and travels into the outfield, usually into one of the corners.

Bullpen. The area, complete with mounds and home plates, where *relief pitchers* warm up with a backup catcher. Never in fair territory, the bullpen is usually located on opposite sides of the outfield. The term bullpen may also refer to the relief pitchers themselves.

Bunched hits. Said of several hits that come together in one inning.

Bunt. (1) *Conventional:* Batter squares around with both feet pointed toward the pitcher, slides one hand halfway up the bat, levels the bat, and taps the ball gently on the ground. (2) *Drag:* As the pitch travels toward the plate, the batter holds his bat out with one or both hands, and begins his running motion toward first base. While he is in stride, the ball strikes the bat and rolls slowly on the ground. (3) *Slash:* The batter squares around as if to bunt, but instead he swings the bat, usually trying to hit the ball past the charging third baseman.
   In any batting maneuver judged by the umpire to be a bunt attempt, the batter is automatically out on a bunt that goes foul if the batter already has two strikes against him. This counts as a strikeout for both the pitcher's and the batter's records.

Bush. (1) Minor semi-professional league. (2) Playing performance or individual behavior unbefitting a professional athlete.

Butterfingers. Derogatory term describing someone who drops or is prone to dropping the ball.

Cactus league. Major league teams that conduct spring training in the Southwest and play each other in *exhibition* games.

Call. (1) The umpire's ruling on a play. (2) The catcher's signal for a specific kind of pitch. (3) The manager's choice of a starting pitcher or his motion to the bullpen for a reliever.

Called strike. A pitch that enters the *strike zone* and is not swung on by the batter.

Calling the ball. A fielder indicates that he wants to catch a fly ball by waving his arms or yelling out to his fellow players, thereby preventing a collision. "Mine" and "I got it" are common expressions for calling the ball.

Can of corn. A fly ball which is very easy to catch.

Cap. The lightweight fabric or plastic hat worn by a player; the team's initials are sewn on the front.

Captain. A player of special ability and leadership, appointed by the manager to exert a certain degree of authority over the other players. He usually presents the lineup card to the umpire prior to a game and may take part in discussion of the ground rules.

Carrying the team. Refers to a player who performs exceptionally well when the rest of the team is playing poorly, or when several key players are injured. Such individual performances can result in enough wins to enable a team to stay in contention for a playoff spot.

Catcher. The defensive player who wears protective gear

and crouches behind home plate to receive throws from the pitcher. He catches pitches and throws from other fielders, tries to gun down runners stealing, and covers bunts among his many duties.

Catcher's box. The rectangular area behind home plate, measuring 43 inches by 8 feet, where the catcher must remain until a pitch is delivered.

Catcher's interference. Refers to any incident where the catcher obstructs the batter's swing, usually by crouching too close to the plate or reaching forward with the mitt and hitting the bat. The batter is awarded first base.

Caught looking. An expression which refers to a batter who is called out on strikes.

Caught napping. An expression referring to a runner who is surprised by a *pickoff* and tagged out.

Caught stealing. Describes the situation in which a runner tries to advance during or after the pitcher's delivery and is tagged out by a fielder who receives the throw from the catcher.

Cellar. Last place in the *standings*.

Center fielder. Usually the fastest and most proficient of the outfielders, he is positioned behind second base, perhaps 30 yards from the back outfield wall.

Chalk. (1) The white substance, sometimes replaced by lime, for marking the foul lines and the batter's and coaches' boxes. (2) Chalk up: to score or mark a tally.

Chalk raiser. A batted ball adjudged to be in *fair territory* because it hits the foul line and scatters chalk dust.

Challenging the hitter. Many pitchers think that the best strategy is to throw the ball in the area of a batter's known strength. Such a strategy is known as challenging the hitter.

Change of pace. A pitcher's slow pitch, thrown after a fast one, or vica versa, to try to confuse the batter. Some pitchers raise their index and middle fingers just prior to release to make the ball float; this is effective in changing the pace. Similar to *letup*.

Change-up. A pitch delivered in an opposite manner from the pitcher's windup. If the windup is rapid, the pitch is slow, and vica versa; or a pitch thrown at an opposite speed from the one which precedes it.

Charging the ball. An infielder takes a few steps toward a batted ball to try to field the ball on a good bounce. Most players do this instinctively to try to make a play as quickly as possible.

Charley horse. A cramp in the arm or leg, resulting from tightening of the muscle after physical exertion.

Chase. To hit a pitcher so well that several runs are scored and he must be replaced by a *reliever*.

Chatter. The rapidly and sporadically spoken encouragement from players to a pitcher or to batters.

Cheating. Refers to a situation when the infielders position themselves closer to a base than usual because of the possibility of an attempted steal or double play.

Check swing. The batter begins to swing but does not follow through with his swing. If the pitch is out of the strike zone, it is still called a ball.

Checking the runner. Refers to a pitcher's glance toward a man on base to see whether he is taking too long a *lead* before delivering the pitch.

Chest protector. A large padded piece of equipment extending from the neck to the waist; worn by both the catcher and the home plate umpire.

Chin music. A humorous expression for the *beanball* or *brush-back* pitch, thrown high and hard to try to intimidate the batter.

Choke. A player's or coach's failure to respond effectively to a crucial game situation.

Choke up. With reference to hitters, to grip the bat with the hands at some distance from the knob at the end of the bat.

Chopping. Swinging downward on a very sharp angle, often resulting in a high bounding ball.

Circus catch. An "acrobatic" maneuver in which a fielder has to leave his feet by jumping or diving to spear the ball.

Circuit clout. A home run.

Classic. (1) The World Series. (2) A play performed seemingly to perfection; or a player with excellent natural skills.

Cleanup. The 4th hitter in the batting order, so called because he is frequently in the position to hit runs in—that is, to clean (empty) the bases (of runners who occupy them).

Clear the bases. To hit a home run with at least one man on base.

Clear the bench. When a team is leading by a large margin, the manager may take his starters out of the game to give them a rest and to give the substitutes a chance to prove themselves.

Cleats. The plastic, metal, or rubber projections on the bottom of a shoe to increase traction; modified in design for artificial surfaces.

Cliff-hanger. A very close game, especially when the score seesaws back and forth.

Clinch. Term used to indicate that a team's won-lost margin has assured it the capture of the pennant and a spot in the playoffs. Or, said of an amateur whose performance in preseason guarantees him a place on the roster.

Clinic. A place where young amateurs can register for a period of instruction in baseball technique offered by professional athletes and/or coaches during the off-season.

Clothesline. A low and very straight *line drive*.

Club. The group of people who draft and sign a team, provide a field, stadium, equipment, and special facilities, and represent the team in matters dealing with the league.

Clubhouse. The facility adjacent to the field where players dress, shower, socialize, and undergo treatment for injuries or chronic conditions.

Clubhouse lawyer. A player who is frequently given to protest against the management or club policies in the company of other players or the press.

Clutch. Describes a crucial hit or defensive gem. A clutch hitter or clutch fielder is one who characteristically may be counted on to perform such plays.

Coach. Any one of a number of assistants to the manager who help to run a team. There are pitching, batting, fielding, and running coaches.

Coaches' boxes. The first and third base coaches must remain within a special area, marked chalklined boxes measuring 5 feet by 20 feet, located 8 feet from the foul lines. If they fail to do so, the batter may be called out.

Coach's interference. If a coach tries to prevent a runner from advancing to second or home by grabbing or standing in the path of the runner, the player is called out.

Cocking. (1) Pulling one's arm back to throw. (2) Describes the batter's dropping his bat slightly and rotating his arms when preparing to hit; cocking the bat in this manner helps the batter to acquire momentum for a stronger swing.

Collar. (1) A player who fails to get a single hit in a game. (2) A player who *chokes,* or fails to respond well to pressure, is said to have a very tight "collar."

Comebacker. A batted ball, usually a grounder, that goes straight back to the pitcher.

Commissioner. The official head of professional baseball who rules on events which affect the dignity and regulations of the sport. He also acts as judicial authority in matters of *appeal.* The office was created as a result of the famous Black Sox scandal, which involved bribery of players to throw a World Series.

Conference. A discussion on the *mound* among defensive players or between the manager and fielders either to determine strategy or to call for a *relief* pitcher.

Connect. To hit the ball squarely and with force.

Contact hitter. One who is content to hit singles consistently rather than trying for the long ball.

Control. A pitcher's ability to throw the ball within the *strike zone.* He has "pinpoint" control when he can throw within a few inches of his target. A "control" pitcher sacrifices speed and *junk* to get the ball over the plate.

Conventional bunt. See *Bunt.*

Corners. (1) The two parallel edges of home plate where the pitcher usually tries to aim his throws. (2) The areas in right and left field where the foul lines meet the wall or fence. (3) The four bases of the *diamond*.

Cortisone. An adrenal hormone injected into a player for a variety of ailments, including chronic knee problems and pitchers' sore arms; provides temporary relief.

Count. The number of balls and strikes on a batter. Spoken, for example, as 2 and 1, which means 2 balls and 1 strike. 3 balls and 2 strikes is called a full count. The number of balls is always indicated before the number of strikes when giving the count.

Courtesy runner. A runner in amateur competition who is permitted to run for a teammate, usually the pitcher, under special circumstances which allow the replaced player to remain in the game.

Cousin. (1) An opposing team that is easily beaten. (2) A particular batter whom a pitcher regularly strikes out. (3) A particular pitcher whom a batter hits frequently. (4) A catcher who can be readily stolen on by a runner.

Cover. (1) In reference to fielders, to stand behind or close beside a base awaiting a throw when a runner is trying to advance or steal. Or, for one fielder to guard a base when the fielder assigned to that base has to move out of his area. (2) The white horsehide on the outside of a baseball.

Cripple. A pitch thrown with a *count* of 3 and 0 or 3 and 1. The pitcher has to throw a strike to avoid walking the batter, and he takes the chance of *grooving* the ball.

Crooked arm. A derogatory expression referring to a southpaw, a left-handed pitcher.

Crossfire. A pitch thrown with a *sidearm* motion; so-called because the ball comes to the plate from the left side of the mound with a right-handed pitcher, and vice versa for a left-hander.

Cross-over. A step used by fielders and runners alike. The lead foot remains planted and pivots as the opposite foot is lifted; one leg comes across the other as the player begins to accelerate.

Cross-over pivot. A fielding maneuver on a double or triple play in which the second baseman touches the base with his left foot and lands with his right on the infield side of second prior to his relay to first.

Crouch. The position of the catcher as he rests on his haunches, balanced on the balls of his feet, behind the plate.

Crowding the plate. Standing as close to the plate as the batter's box allows. The hitter may be batting defensively, trying to *rattle* the pitcher, or encouraging an inside pitch.

Crown. A term emblematic of a team championship or individual honors, such as the *batting title*.

Cup. A small and durable piece of equipment, made of plastic or thin metal, covered with rubber or moulding, held in place by an athletic supporter to protect a player's genitals.

Cup of coffee. A very brief tryout with a Major League team cut short because the club loses interest or the player gives a poor performance or he suffers injury.

Curfew. The specific time of the evening by which players must be in their quarters, as determined by the team's manager.

Curve. An *off-speed* pitch that is thrown with a sudden outward twist of the wrist and calculated to veer down and away from a batter who hits from the same side that the pitcher throws from.

Cut. (1) A batter's swing. (2) Either to drop a player from the team with an unconditional release, or to demote him to the minors. (3) To hit the inside or outside corner with a pitch.

Cut-off. (1) Maneuver by which an outfielder catches or knocks the ball down before it can travel for extra bases. (2) Cut-off man: an infielder who relays a throw from the outfield.

Cy Young Award. An honor given annually to the pitcher in each league considered the best individual performer on the basis of his *won-lost percentage* and his *earned run average*.

Cycle. Refers to the rare occurrence when a batter hits a single, a double, a triple, and a home run in one game.

Dead. (1) Hands: In reference to the batter who swings from a rigid position rather than allowing his hands to roll backwards. (2) Hit: Refers to a ball that is batted weakly.

Dead ball. A batted or thrown ball that bounces over a field barrier or into the stands or dugout, stopping action in the game pending a ruling by the umpire. Certain areas on the field may also be ruled "dead" because of possible injury to a fielder.

Deck. (1) A division of seats in a stadium—sometimes called a tier, and referred to as lower, upper, and upper upper. (2) To hit a batter with a pitch.

Defense. Refers simply to the team in the field or the entirety of the strategy which they employ, such as an infield *shift,* a *pitchout,* or a *pickoff*.

Delayed steal. Occurs when a runner, perceiving that a fielder is not alert or is not covering his base after a pitch, waits until the ball is returned to the pitcher before he tries to advance.

Delivery. The passage of the ball from the pitcher toward home plate. The entire motion, from windup to release, of a pitcher throwing the ball.

Derby. A game that resembles baseball but is played on a much narrower field with fewer players. Batters do not run the bases; any grounder or fly ball which is caught is an out; and all hits are automatic and are determined by whatever rules are established.

Designated hitter. In the American League, the player who regularly bats for the pitcher. He does not play defense, and the pitcher remains in the game. In the National League, only a *pinch hitter* may bat for the pitcher, who is then relieved.

Diamond. The infield area, representing a square with 90-foot sides. The four corners are the bases, with first base diagonally to the right and third base diagonally to the left of home plate. The term diamond may also refer to the entire field. (See Appendix, pp. 93, 94.)

Dig in. In reference to the action of the batter, to scrape the dirt away in the batter's box and twist into the soil to keep his back foot firmly anchored when he swings.

Dime player. An infielder who doesn't hustle after a ball hit behind or to either side of him. He usually also fails to back up throws and to get into position for a cut-off.

Disabled. An injured player who must remain on the disabled list for a specified period of time (either 15 or 21 days) when he is replaced by another player on the roster.

Dish. Another word for *home plate,* the five-sided slab of rubber behind which the catcher and umpire crouch, and beside which the batter stands.

Distance to stands. There is usually 60 feet of space between home plate and the backstop, and between first and third base to the stands.

Division. Both the National and American leagues are divided into two sections, East and West. The leagues do not play each other in regular season games. However, all of the teams within a league compete, and winners of each section meet in the *playoffs*.

Doctoring the ball. An expression which refers to a pitcher's doing something unnatural and illegal to the ball to get it to *move*. In addition to using the spitball, some pitchers cut the ball with rings or cleats on their spikes.

Dogging. (1) A fielder's backing off from a batted ball because he is afraid of it. (2) Generally, failure of any player to give his best.

Double. A two-base *hit*. The batter reaches second base safely after hitting the ball in fair territory and no error is committed by a fielder.

Double hit. Occurs when the batter, having hit the ball, throws his bat and again hits the batted ball rolling in fair territory; he is out.

Double off. When a line drive or fly ball is caught, putting the batter out, and the fielder catching the ball throws to a base previously occupied by a runner who has not *tagged up*, the runner is out and is said to be doubled off.

Double play. Occurs whenever two offensive players are put out on the same play. The batter is usually one of the two involved. Most occur on grounders to the infield or when a liner is speared and a runner is caught off base.

Double play depth. The positions assumed by the fielders, especially the second baseman and the shortstop, who move closer to second base in situations involving one or no previous outs and offensive runners occupying one or more bases.

Double steal. Two runners try to *steal* simultaneously;

especially important when first and third are occupied. The runner on first tries for second and, if the catcher makes a throw, the runner on third tries for home.

Doubleheader. Two games played in succession, usually by the same teams, with about a twenty minute intermission.

Down the cock. Another expression for a perfectly *grooved* pitch.

Down the pipe. An expression which refers to a pitch thrown over the heart of the plate.

Draft. The process by which college and Minor League players are chosen by a particular team. When veterans have played out their options, they can also be drafted by many teams.

Drag bunt. See *Bunt.*

Drill. (1) Any of a number of exercises designed to develop or refine particular skills, such as bunting, hit-and-run, the quarterback drill, rundowns, and the double steal. (2) To hit a ball very hard.

Drive. To hit a ball a long distance, especially on a line.

Drive in. To hit a run in; that is, to enable a base runner to score by virtue of the batter's accomplishment.

Drop. An overhand pitch that sinks suddenly in front of the plate; any pitch, such as the forkball or spitter, which veers downward.

Drunk. A term expressing the condition of the bases when they're loaded—that is, when first, second, and third base are occupied by offensive runners.

Dugout. A shelter for each team containing a bench where the players and coaches sit. It is usually cut underground and situated on either side of the diamond, and usually has a passageway leading to the clubhouse.

Dummy signals. Refers to the coach's use of different positions or stances for each signal; for example, standing at the front or back of the box, or standing with his legs crossed.

Duster. (1) A brush-back pitch that sends the batter into the dirt. (2) A *slide*.

Early swing. A batter's swing at a ball far out in front of the plate; an early swing usually misses the ball altogether, or causes the ball to go foul when contact is made.

Earned run. One for which the pitcher is responsible. If an error contributes to a run or prolongs an inning, subsequent runs are unearned.

Earned run average (ERA). A pitcher's most important statistic, along with his *won-lost* record. To calculate the earned run average, *earned runs* are divided by the number of innings pitched, then multiplied by 9. For example, if a pitcher goes 8 innings and gives up 3 earned runs, his ERA is $3 \div 8 = .375 \times 9 = 3.38$.

Ejection. When a player or coach violates a rule or conducts himself in an unsportsmanlike manner, the umpire may remove him from the game.

Emery ball. A baseball doctored by the pitcher with emery cloth, making the rough side more subject to the force of air, causing the ball to *"move"* as it approaches the plate.

Emigré. A player who moves from one team to another.

Equipment. (1) The paraphernalia used in a game, such as bats, balls, gloves, helmets, and the catcher's gear. (2) The pitcher's arsenal of weapons, or any player's particular skills.

Equipment manager. The club official who oversees the purchase and transport of a team's gear.

Error. Occurs when a fielder misses a batted ball he could readily have caught, or when he makes a wild throw causing a runner to be safe. An error is so determined by the official scorer.

Ethyl chloride. A cold gaseous spray that freezes an injured bone or muscle, reducing pain and allowing a player to remain in the game. Commonly employed when a batter has been physically struck by a pitched ball.

Exhibition games. Unofficial games played during the preseason to prepare the teams for their long schedule.

Expansion. An additional franchise is permitted by the league officials to enter the league. Players are pooled from a special draft imposed on existing teams, exempting only the starters, and a number of pitchers and substitutes.

Extra bases. Since most hits are singles, any double, triple, or home run is considered "extra" and is figured in terms of total bases in a *slugging percentage*.

Extra innings. Played until one team wins when a game is tied after its regular duration of nine innings.

Eye. Term for a particular batter's ability to differentiate between balls and strikes, often more a matter of discipline than eyesight.

"Eyes" on it. An expression referring to a hit that barely escapes the reach of the fielders, as if it had a mind of its own.

Face mask. A protective piece of equipment made of wire or metal and canvas straps; worn by the catcher and the home plate umpire.

Fadeaway. Refers to the pitcher's motion when he falls off of the *mound* after his *delivery;* especially characteristic of the screwballer, because of the difficult arm motion.

Fair territory. The area within the 90-degree angle formed by the foul lines; extends from the foul lines running from home plate, along third and first base, to the foul poles located at the end of the outfield. The foul lines themselves and the foul poles are considered part of fair territory.

Fan. (1) A spectator at a game or an avid follower of a team. (2) To strike out.

Farm. A Minor League team associated with a Major League club. The parent club may send castoffs to the farm to work on their weaknesses, and may recall them at any time.

Fastball. The most common pitch, thrown on a relatively even trajectory at full velocity.

Fear. Generally recognized as the pervasive psychological condition of the batter, since fastballs travel at velocities up to about 100 mph. It could be said that fear is mastered but never really totally overcome by the successful hitter.

Fence buster. A power hitter; the term derives from the era when the home run barrier was almost always a wooden fence.

Field. The playing area in general, including fair and foul territory. On most professional fields, the minimum distance from home plate to the right and left field foul poles is 325 feet, and 400 feet to dead center. (See Appendix, p. 94.)

Fielder. There are 3 outfielders and 4 infielders who chase batted balls and try to make *put-outs.* The pitcher and catcher, who combine to make the *battery,* are not usually called fielders.

Fielder's choice. The fielder's option to play for a *force-out,* getting the runner on the base paths rather than the batter at first.

Fielding. A defensive player's catch or attempt to catch a batted ball. Infielders usually stand bent over, balanced on the balls of their feet, with gloves dangling a few inches above the playing surface. Outfielders are more relaxed, but must be ready to move sideways or backward very quickly and simultaneously judge the distance of the ball.

Fifty-eight footer. While the distance from the pitcher's mound to home plate is 60 feet 6 inches, this expression is used by a catcher to describe a pitch that hits the dirt, regardless of how far it actually travels.

Fireballer. A fastballer; a pitcher who uses the *fastball* as his primary pitch.

Fireman of the Year Award. The *relief* pitcher is often called a "fireman"; this honor is conferred to the best relievers in both the National and American leagues.

First base coach. His role is primarily to instruct the runner on first on what to do in any given situation. He may also relay signals to the batter or to the runner on second.

First baseman. An infielder positioned on the right side of the diamond near first base. His duties include holding the runner close to the base, fielding bunts, guarding the line against extra base hits, and receiving relays from other infielders for put-outs at first.

First string. The starting lineup.

Flash. A signal given once and very quickly; for example, by tipping the hat or tugging on the belt.

Flat. As opposed to "live," a pitch that comes in very straight and is usually easy to hit.

Fly ball. A batted ball that leaves the bat on a relatively high trajectory, ascending up into the air.

Follow-through. (1) The final stage of a pitcher's motion after he has delivered the ball, with arm and body still in motion. (2) Also, the end of a batter's swing when he brings the bat all the way around.

Foot-in-the-bucket. Describes the batter who steps from the ball rather than toward it, usually from fear of being hit.

Force-in. When the pitcher walks a batter with bases loaded, the runner on third freely advances across the plate for a run; that is, he is forced in.

Force-out. Occurs when a player is compelled to advance to a base and the fielder steps on the bag to get him out. If first is occupied, the runner must go to second when the ball is batted fairly and not caught on a fly. Correspondingly, if first and second or all bases are occupied, each runner is forced to the next base.

Forfeit. A game officially scored 9-0 by the umpire against the team that exhibits aberrant behavior. This may occur when not enough players take the field; when a team takes an excessive amount of time taking the field, coming to bat, conferring at the mound, changing pitchers, etc.; when a team refuses to comply with an umpire's ruling (for example, when someone is ejected); or when partisan fans get out of control.

Forkball. A type of pitch in which the pitcher's middle and index fingers are spread out to either side of the ball, limiting the spin and causing the pitch to flutter.

Foul ball. Any ball hit outside of *fair territory*. If caught on the fly, it is still an out.

Foul lines. The (usually) chalk lines extending from home plate, along besides first and third base, to the outfield foul poles. The foul lines, themselves in fair territory, demark the fair territory of the entire infield and outfield.

Foul poles. Brightly painted poles which extend up above the field, perpendicular to the foul lines, at the home run barrier. A batted ball that strikes the foul pole and then bounces back onto the outfield is a home run.

Foul territory. The area outside the 90-degree angle formed by the *foul lines.* The ball is still playable unless it goes in an area designated "dead."

Foul tip. Occurs when the ball hits the edge of the bat and is only slightly deflected from its natural trajectory. If caught by the catcher when there are 2 strikes on the batter, the batter is out. The ball must hit the catcher's glove if bobbled and held, however, before striking his equipment or part of his body.

Four-bagger. A home run.

Free agent. A player whose contract has expired. He is free to negotiate with any team, including his own.

Free ticket. A *walk;* so called because the batter does not even have to swing to get aboard.

Front office. The jurisdiction of the general manager who is responsible for business and personnel, including coming to terms with players on their contracts and deciding on trades.

Full count. See *Count.*

Fungo. A very long, thin bat used by a coach for hitting infield and outfield practice. Its size and its light weight enable its user to direct practice hits more accurately.

Fungo circles. Two circles on the field, near home plate, where fungo hitters usually stand.

Games back. The total number of games that a team must win or that the first place team must lose so that the lower team can assume first place. For example, if a team is 3 games back, it must win 3 games while the first place team loses 3; or win 6 games while the first place team doesn't play; or any combination thereof. Each victory and each loss counts as ½ of a game.

Gap. (1) A team's weakness. (2) The large space between the outfielders where extra-base hits often travel.

General manager. The coordinator of business and personnel for a club whose authority is given him by the owners, including the power to sign players and coaches and conduct trades.

Give up. (1) For a pitcher to surrender a walk, hit, or run. (2) With a man on first, the batter hits the ball to the right side of the infield to sacrifice the runner to second.

Glass arm. An expression which refers primarily to pitchers, connoting an easily strained or injured arm.

Glove. A flexible piece of leather equipment used to facilitate catching by all fielders except the first baseman and catcher, whose "gloves" are more properly termed *mitts*.

"Gnat's eyelash." An expression describing a very close play; for example, on a tag or on a ball that is barely fair or foul.

Going the distance. Refers to a pitcher throwing a complete game, without being relieved, whether he wins or loses.

Going to the mouth. If a pitcher does so—puts his fingertips to his lips or mouth—when standing on the mound, he may be ejected from the game; he must walk down to the field surface to make the move legal. Going to the mouth arouses suspicion of the spitball.

Going with the pitch. Hitting the ball to the side of the plate where it is pitched. A pitch on the outside corner for a right-handed batter is hit to right field.

Gold Glove Award. Presented annually to Major League players who have distinguished themselves defensively by being selected to the National and American league all-star fielding teams.

Golf ball. The batter manages to hit a very low pitch, often resulting in a fly ball since he must swing upward.

Good wood. An expression referring to solid contact between the bat and the ball.

Gopher ball. A long hit, especially a home run.

Grab. To make a catch.

Grand slam. A home run with the bases loaded (three men on the bases), resulting in four runs being scored.

Grandstand. All of the seats in a stadium protected from the weather by a roof.

Grandstand manager. A rambunctious fan who tries to direct the team and the manager from the stands.

Grandstander. A flashy player who shows off his talents, but is now regarded and used with greater tolerance with the emphasis on the "entertainment" value of baseball.

Grapefruit league. Major League teams that conduct spring training in Florida and play each other in *exhibition games.*

Grease ball. One version of the spitter *(spitball)* where the pitcher uses a petroleum jelly or some other sticky substance to offset the ball's normal trajectory.

Green light. Refers to the coach signalling the batter that he may swing when he would ordinarily *take;* for example, when the count is 3 and 0.

Grip. (1) The manner in which a pitcher holds the ball. For most pitches, he will have his index and middle fingers on top of the ball across the seam and the other fingers tucked underneath the ball. (2) A batter's grasp on the bat when he is at the plate. If he is right-handed, his left or "meat" hand will be situated nearest to the knob, and vice versa if he is left-handed.

Groove. (1) A pitch down the center of the plate, usually about waist-high. (2) A player's most comfortable and effective level and style of play.

Ground crew. The men who are responsible for total maintenance and preparation of the field. Their duties include covering the infield with tarpaulin when it rains, cutting the grass or cleaning the turf, chalking the foul lines and boxes before a game, and sweeping the infield periodically during the game.

Ground rule hit. Applies to a situation when something unusual happens to a batted ball. If the ball bounces over the fence or wall, it is an automatic double. When the ball bounces onto the field off the scoreboard, it may be a double or home run depending on the field. The ball may also bounce into the stands, etc., and specific rules are used.

Ground rules. Guidelines related by the home team manager to the visiting manager and the umpire prior to a game, pertaining to special stipulations made necessary by the peculiar dimensions of the field.

Grounder. Any ball hit on the ground with the exception of a *bunt* or *smash*.

Guessing. An expression which characterizes the dynamics of the struggle between the pitcher and batter: the hitter is trying to guess what will be thrown while the pitcher is preparing to throw something else.

Hall of Fame. In 1939 in Cooperstown, New York, a building was dedicated as a baseball museum. It houses an extensive collection of baseball memorabilia as well as bronze plaques of great players inducted into the Hall for their outstanding careers and qualities of sportsmanship. Presently, players must be retired 5 years before being eligible and are selected by secret ballot. Deceased players are chosen by a special committee.

Handcuff. The restriction of the movement of a fielder's glove hand when a grounder bounces up very quickly or a sharply hit ball comes very close to his body.

Handle. (1) The narrowest part of the bat above the knob where the hitter grips the bat. (2) An expression referring to a player's attempt to get hold of a ball he has bobbled or one that is hit very hard and handcuffs him.

Hanging curve. Instead of breaking down and away, this pitch hardly breaks at all and hangs in the air, an easy target for an opportunistic hitter.

Hammer. To hit the ball very hard, especially on a line; or to hit an opposing pitcher very well in a game.

Have an idea. The admonition of a coach to his players to get them to think or concentrate on the playing field when they have been making mental errors.

Hawk. A fleet-footed outfielder who has excellent reflexes and can chase a ball down in virtually any part of his territory.

Heel. The bottom of the inside of the glove near the wrist and the least flexible part.

Helmet. A protective hat made of plastic or synthetic fiber worn by hitters.

High. A pitch above the *letters* which mark the top of the strike zone; a *ball,* unless swung on by the batter.

High-ball hitter. A batter known for his tendency to hit pitches above the waist more consistently than lower pitches.

Hill. The *mound,* a circular projection of firmly packed dirt on top of which the pitcher's *rubber* is imbedded. It can be no higher than 10 inches and no wider than 18 feet in diameter.

Hit. (1) A batted ball that travels in *fair territory,* allowing the batter to reach base safely without an error being committed. (2) Any batted ball.

Hit by pitch. Unless a batter leans in to a pitch or fails to get out of the way by his own negligence, he is awarded first base. If he is hit intentionally, the pitcher may be ejected from the game.

Hit-and-run. An offensive play in which one or more runners advance toward the next base during the pitcher's delivery, while the batter tries to get a hit, preferably on the ground so that the runner(s) is not caught off.

Hitching. Refers to the batter's dropping his hands suddenly before a pitch is delivered, usually throwing his timing off and causing the ball to pop up.

Hitter. See *Batter.*

Hitting a ton. An expression referring to a batter who is on a tear, hitting consistently from game to game.

Holding a runner. With a runner on first base and second base unoccupied, the first baseman stands directly beside the bag on the home plate side facing the pitcher and awaits a possible pickoff move.

Holdout. A player who misses part of spring training or the early part of the season because he wants more money for signing a contract than the club is offering.

Home plate. A five-sided piece of white rubber, 17 inches long and 12 inches wide. The catcher and umpire crouch behind it; its width is also the width of the strike zone. The batter stands beside the plate in his box and runners who score must reach home safely.

Home run. A four-base *hit.* A batter hits the ball over the wall or fence in fair territory; it does not matter if the ball goes foul after it has passed the foul pole. Or, the batter hits the ball fairly and reaches home without an error being committed—called an inisde-the-park home run.

Home run cut. A very full swing of a batter going for the fences. Most hitters do not make solid contact when they overswing in this way, but rather hit most of their homers with a normal swing.

Home run derby. A game in which only a few players participate. They compete to see who can hit the most home runs, and any other hit is considered an out.

Home run king. The player in each league who has the most homers by the end of the season; or the player with the most in baseball history.

Home team. The team that invites another team to compete on its field. The *visiting team* bats first, but the home team has the final chance to score.

Homer. A four-base *hit:* a *home run.*

Homestand. A series of consecutive games played by a team against one or more visiting teams on its home field. The schedule is arranged so that teams can play as many games as possible before going on the road.

Homestretch. The last month of the season, when teams in contention for the playoffs battle for the pennant.

Hook. The tendency of a manager to call for a reliever at the first sign of trouble for the pitcher in the game.

Hook slide. A runner approaches a base and slides feet first, tucking one leg under him. He hooks the opposite leg so that his foot catches the side or one corner of the bag.

Hop. (1) The bounce of a ground ball. (2) The apparent jumping motion of a very fast pitch. This occurs because gravity has less of an effect on the ball. It is illusory and based on the fact that most pitches descend gradually in their flight to the plate rather than coming in on a level trajectory.

Hose. The arm of a player, especially the pitcher.

Hot corner. An expression referring to the third baseman's position because he stands within close proximity to the batter and must frequently rely on his reflexes.

Hot dogging. Exhibiting flashy play or showing off. Some observers look upon this behavior with scorn; others defend it, saying that it adds more to the entertainment value of the sport.

Hugging. A fielder staying very close to the bag. First and third basemen do so when a *pull hitter* comes up who hits to their side, or in the late innings when they want to protect against extra-base hits.

Hummingbird ass. A player who criticizes or jibes other players but who lacks the courage to back up his taunts.

Hung up. Caught between two bases. Pertaining to base runners, this may occur on a line drive caught by a fielder where the runner has not tagged up; on an unsuccessful hit-and-run; on a pickoff where the runner is "caught napping"; etc. Being hung up may result in a *force-out* or a *rundown*.

Hurler. A pitcher.

Hurrying the throw. On bunts, slow rollers, Baltimore chops, bobbles, and balls hit into the hole (between the third baseman and shortstop), the fielder may have to throw quickly to get the runner out.

Illegal pitch. Occurs when the pitcher makes his delivery with his foot off the *rubber;* when he throws a *quick* return pitch or commits a *balk;* or when he throws a *spitball* or any doctored pitch.

Import. A girlfriend or wife brought on a road trip by a player or coach.

In play. Refers to any ball that is not "dead," especially a playable foul pop or a fair ball that bounces on the foul side of the line after it passes first or third base.

In the hole. (1) The gap between the third baseman and the shortstop where the shortstop ranges for some of his more difficult plays; or any gap between 2 fielders. (2) Refers to the batter scheduled to follow the batter who is *on deck.*

Indicator. The umpire's hand-held mechanism for keeping track of the number of balls, strikes, outs, and runs scored.

Infield fly rule. If first and second are occupied and there are none or one out, any fly ball in the infield is automatically ruled an out. This prevents a fielder from missing the ball intentionally to set up a force-out.

Infield hit. Occurs when a batted ball is fielded but the hitter reaches base safely, usually because he has good speed.

Infield up. A defensive situation in which the infielders position themselves closer to the batter, usually within the base paths, in order to cut down a runner trying to advance from third to home.

Infielder. One of four fielders who occupy the infield, not including the pitcher and catcher: the first and second basemen, the shortstop, and the third baseman.

Injured reserve. An injured player who may nevertheless be reinstated at any time because he has not been replaced on the *roster.*

Inner-squad game. A game played according to regular rules among players on the same team for practice.

Inning. Each team's opportunity to complete a turn at bat. Each team gets to hit until 3 put-outs are made, for a total of 6. Nine innings constitute a standard game unless the home team is ahead in the 9th in which case 8½ innings suffice.

Inside. A pitch out of the *strike zone* on the side of the plate closest to the batter.

Inside baseball. That crucial area of the sport which involves techniques of base-running, sacrificing, stealing, and the hit-and-run and run-and-hit.

Inside pivot. A defensive maneuver in which the shortstop brushes the bag with his foot on the home plate side of the base prior to his relay to first on a *double play.*

Inside-out swing. The batter's hands are ahead of the bat when he hits the ball, causing the ball to go to the opposite field. This occurs if the batter swings when the pitch is almost past him.

Inside-the-park home run. A four-base hit occurring in fair territory; the ball does not go over the wall or fence, but the batter manages to complete a circuit of the bases on the hit without an error being committed.

Intentional walk. The pitcher walks a batter on purpose if he is a dangerous hitter and men are on base; or when an extra-base hit would be particularly crucial; or when first base is "open" and the defense wants to set up a double play.

Interference. Refers to a situation where a runner obstructs a fielder who is trying to make a play; the runner is called out. For example, if a fielder stands in the baseline awaiting a batted ball, the runner must avoid a collision. Other kinds of interference may affect the catcher, coach, or fielder.

Interference at first base. If the runner collides with the first baseman when he is receiving the throw on the inside of the foul line, the runner is out. If he collides with the fielder on the foul side of the line, he is awarded first base.

Iron man. A very durable player, especially a pitcher who can throw for many innings without tiring.

Iron mike. The pitching machine used frequently during batting practice, helping to preserve the strength of the pitching staff.

Ivory. An amateur player who has exceptional skills and is observed by a scout or a manager during a game or tryout.

Jam. To pitch the ball *inside* to intimidate the batter or to try to prevent him from taking a full swing.

Jersey. The article of clothing worn under the shirt, with sleeves that match the uniform in color.

Jockey. A player who taunts either the opposing team or a particular player from the opposing bench.

Jockstrap. An athletic supporter, the elastic piece of equipment worn around a player's waist for protection of the groin.

Journeyman. An experienced player who does not have exceptional skill but is consistent in his play. He may not be a starter, but he is kept on the roster for his steadiness.

Jug handle. A *curve ball* with such a wide arc that it sweeps across the plate; often thrown with a *sidearm* delivery.

Juiced. An expression referring to a ball hit very hard or for long distance.

Junk. The whole arsenal of *off-speed pitches* like the curve, forkball, drop, slider, and knuckler.

Jump. The running start taken by a base runner during the pitcher's windup, or by a fielder when he starts toward the ball at the crack of the bat.

Jumping. Leaving the team suddenly and without permission. The player is usually fined by the manager for such an action.

K. The abbreviation frequently used in place of "SO" to designate a strikeout.

Keep him honest. A directive to a pitcher to throw strikes to a batter in order to make him hit or get on base rather than allowing him a free ticket by a walk.

Keystone. A term which refers to the second baseman's position because he is involved in so many crucial plays. For example, the second baseman must cover first on a bunt, cover second on a steal or a double play, and relay throws in from the outfield.

Kick. After the pitcher brings his arms down to about waist level during his windup, he raises one leg, sometimes above the waist.

Kicking it out. When a bunt or slow roller is in foul territory but is very close to the foul line, a fielder may kick it foul to make sure that it doesn't roll fair before it gets to the bag. Such a move is good defense, as the batter would be likely to reach first safely on a ball so hit.

Kicks. The spikes or cleats on the bottom of baseball shoes that can cause an injury, especially when a runner slides into a base.

Kill the ball. A batter's attempt to hit a long drive, usually resulting in an overswing and loss of eye contact with the ball.

Knob. The lip on the end of the bat handle that keeps the bat from slipping out of the hitter's hands. Most power hitters grip the bat at the knob rather than *choke up*.

Knockdown. A brush-back pitch that forces the batter to hit the dirt; if the umpire judges the pitch an intended *beanball,* the pitcher may be ejected from the game.

Knocked out of the box. An expression referring to a pitcher who has been relieved after having given up a barrage of hits.

Knuckle baller. A pitcher who relies primarily on his *knuckler.* A good knuckler is very difficult to hit and the pitch itself exerts very little strain on the pitcher's arm.

Knuckler (knuckle ball). A type of pitch where the pitcher grips the ball with either his knuckles or fingertips. The ball has very little spin and may move around in an unpredictable fashion because of its resistance to air currents.

Law. The legal code for the sport of baseball determining criteria for such matters as signing contracts, trading, or waiving a player. It is enacted and modified collectively by the club owners.

Lay one down. A directive to the batter to *bunt.* The directive is given by the coach either by a signal or by word of mouth.

Lead. The runner edges, or leads, his way off base so that he has less distance to travel should he attempt to advance on a hit or sacrifice, or by stealing. Most good runners take leads by shuffling off the base rather than using cross-over steps which would be dangerous footing in case of an attempted pickoff.

Lead bat. A bat which has had a hole drilled in it and has been filled with lead or some other heavy metal; for practice swung by an *on-deck* hitter to make the bat seem lighter when he comes to the plate.

Leadoff. (1) The first batter in the lineup, usually the most consistent hitter on the team and generally a fast runner as well. (2) The first batter in either half of an inning.

League. A major structural division of any baseball program. The Majors are comprised of two such groups and each one is composed of two divisions, East and West. The National and American Leagues do not compete against one another in regular season play, but meet only in the *All Star Game* and the *World Series*.

National	**American**
East	*East*
Chicago Cubs	Baltimore Orioles
Montreal Expos	Boston Red Sox
New York Mets	Cleveland Indians
Philadelphia Phillies	Detroit Tigers
Pittsburgh Pirates	Milwaukee Brewers
St. Louis Cardinals	New York Yankees
West	*West*
Atlanta Braves	California Angels
Cincinnati Reds	Chicago White Sox
Houston Astros	Kansas City Royals
Los Angeles Dodgers	Minnesota Twins
San Diego Padres	Oakland Athletics
San Francisco Giants	Texas Rangers

The American League teams Toronto Bluejays (East) and Seattle Mariners (West) are expansion teams.

Leaning. Some runners lean toward the next base when taking a lead. This provides an advantage if they want to advance or steal by giving them a quicker jump; however, it makes it more difficult to get back to the bag on an attempted pickoff.

Left fielder. The outfielder positioned near the left foul line. He is usually the outfielder with the weakest arm since his throw to third is the shortest.

Left on base (LOB). The number of men stranded on base when the third out has been made in an inning.

Left out. A rather derogatory expression, heard primarily on sandlots and among amateur players in general, referring to the left fielder, whose position is often considered least important. This is because amateurs have a tendency to push the ball to right field rather than pull it to left (when speaking of right-handed hitters).

Left-center. The gap in the outfield between the left and center fielders.

Leg it out. Pertaining to runners, to beat a throw to a base, particularly on an infield hit.

Legal game. A game that lasts 5 innings, or 4½ when the home team is ahead, constitutes a full game and occurs in the event of darkness, rain, extreme cold, or other bad conditions which by decision of the umpire warrant termination of the game.

Letters. The top extremity of the strike zone is the batter's armpits, which are approximately in line with the letters of his team's name printed on his shirt.

Letup. An *off-speed pitch* thrown after a fastball; a slow *change-up*.

Limit. A maximum of 25 players can remain on the active *roster* from one month after the season begins to September 1.

Line drive. A ball that leaves the bat on a fairly even trajectory, usually at high velocity. A player who can hit line drives frequently is exceptional.

Line out. A defensive play in which a *line drive* is caught by a fielder for a put-out.

Lineup. The list of starting players on each team presented to the umpire before each game. Players are designated in their batting order.

Little League. A federally authorized organization, funded largely by local business, dedicated to youths between the ages of 8 and 12. The dimensions of the field differ, of course, from those of the Major Leagues.
Field: Two-thirds the size of the Majors.
Distance between bases: 60 feet instead of 90.
Distance of mound to plate: 46 feet instead of 60 feet, 6 inches.
Home run distance: 180 feet down both foul lines; 200 feet to dead center.
Batter's box: 66 inches by 3 feet.
Coach's box: 8 feet by 4 feet, situated 6 feet from the baseline.

Live. An expression describing a pitch that rises, sinks, floats, flutters, moves in toward the batter, or out away from him; or a fastball that has a "hop."

Loaded. Refers to a situation where all three bases are occupied by runners. A home run with the bases loaded is called a grand slam.

Lob. A casual or soft throw, sometimes necessary in a game when two fielders are very close to each other.

Lollipop. A soft pitch or throw. The pitch may be an attempt to fool the batter; the throw may be made necessary because two fielders are so close together.

Long ball. A very deep hit; if not caught, it will almost always enable the batter to go for extra bases.

Long count. A *count* of 3 balls and 2 strikes on the batter; also called a full count.

Long relief. Refers to a *bullpen* pitcher who comes in early in a game and is expected to go the route (that is, finish the game.) Some relievers specialize in this type situation.

Look. To take—that is, not swing at—a pitch. When a batter "looks for a walk," he is waiting for the pitcher to throw a *ball (1)*.

Loop. (1) A league. (2) A fly ball hit not too high in the air.

Losing pitcher. The hurler on the losing team who is responsible for the opposition's tally which ultimately decides the game. If a pitcher leaves the game with his team tied or ahead, and there are men on base who eventually score enough runs to reverse the lead, the pitcher is still charged with a loss.

Low. A pitch below the knees, which are the bottom mark of the strike zone. A low pitch is a *ball,* unless swung on by the batter.

Low-ball hitter. A batter known for his ability to hit pitches low in the strike zone most effectively.

Lumber. The bat, whether it is made of ash or willow or some other kind of wood.

Lunge. A jerky, forward motion in a batter's attempt to hit a ball whose trajectory he has misjudged, causing him to reach far out in front of the plate in order to make contact.

Major Leagues. The highest echelon of professional baseball, comprising the National and American leagues, each of which is broken down into an East and West division. See under *League*.

Manager. A man experienced in baseball who is appointed by the owners to run the team. Ideally, he has full authority over the lineup, game strategy, and the behavior of his players. In amateur play, managers are hired or appointed in a much less formal manner.

Meat. (1) The thickest part of the bat, measuring as much as 2¾ inches in diameter. (2) The strongest hitters in the lineup, usually batting second through fifth in the lineup.

Meat hand. The hand closest to the *knob* of the bat when the batter takes his grip.

Meeting the ball. Swinging the bat while the ball is still out in front of the plate in order to connect properly with the pitched ball.

Men in blue. Term referring to the *umpires*.

Mental error. A mistake caused by forgetfulness or some other mental letdown rather than a physical error or muff. For example, on a grounder to the second baseman with a runner advancing from first to second, he throws to first for a put-out instead of to second for the force-out and possible double play.

Minors. The professional leagues just below the Majors, generally sponsored and controlled by a Major League club. The three levels are AAA, AA, and A. The triple A is composed of the American Association, the International League, and the Pacific Coast League.

Misjudge. For a fielder to run in on a fly ball over his head or stay back on a shallow hit; or to run too hard and cross over the path of the ball so that it lands at his back.

Missing the bag. For runners, bypassing a base without stepping on it. If the opposition notices this aberration, they can get the runner out: the pitcher winds up from the *stretch* and throws the ball to a fielder who touches the base which the base runner had missed.

Mistake hitter. A batter who reacts well after he has been fooled by a pitch. For example, he may stride too soon on a change-up and still have his bat in control to hit the ball.

Mitt. May refer to any glove, but usually means the first baseman's and catcher's gloves specifically. The catcher's is heavily padded and has only two slots for fingers, one for the thumb and the other for the rest of the hand. The first baseman uses a more flexible mitt, which may have three finger slots or more.

Mixing it up. When a pitcher throws many different kinds of pitches, and throws them low, high, inside, and outside to try to keep the batter guessing, he is said to be mixing it up.

Moss. Slang word for a player's hair.

Most Valuable Player (MVP). The player in the National and American League considered the best individual performer and greatest asset to his team's success during the year. Judged by the sports writers.

Motor. To run at top speed.

Mound. The elevated, circular hill of dirt on top of which the pitching rubber is imbedded. It should be no higher than 10 inches and no more than 18 feet in diameter.

"Moves." An expression referring to a "live" pitch because it always has some kind of movement, such as curving, rising, or dropping.

Moving the ball around. A pitcher's strategy of aiming his throws to a different target—low, high, inside, outside—on practically every pitch.

Muff. A fielding error such as dropping a fly ball or grounder, or mishandling a relay throw.

Nab. To tag or throw a runner out, especially when he is trying to steal or stretch a hit for extra bases.

Nail. To throw a runner out when he is trying to steal or advance on a batted ball.

National League. See *League*.

Night cap. The second game of a doubleheader when it is played in the evening.

Night games. Played under bright lights, they are nowadays more frequent than day games in the Major Leagues in order to attract the day-working fans.

Nine. A term used for a baseball team. Refers particularly to the starting lineup, as in the "starting nine."

Nod. Signifies the manager's decision to start a particular pitcher after some deliberation.

No-hitter. A complete game in which the pitcher does not surrender a single *hit* to the opposition. This most unusual feat is a great pitching triumph (although, because of errors, walks, etc., it is always possible that a pitcher may throw a no-hitter and still lose the game).

Obstruction. A fielder's interference with a runner. If a fielder in the baseline is not awaiting a batted ball and he collides with a runner, the runner is awarded a base.

Offense. Refers simply to the team at bat or the strategies which they use, such as the *take,* the *bunt,* the *hit-and-run,* and the *suicide squeeze,* to name a few.

Official scorer. A newspaper reporter chosen by the league President to record statistics for a Major League game. He also decides on hits and errors in situations when the distinction between a hit and an error is not clear-cut.

Off-speed pitch. Any pitch thrown at less than full velocity. Breaking pitches—such as the *curve, slider, forkball, screwball* and *knuckler*—cannot be thrown like a fastball.

Old-cat. A somewhat obsolete term for a pick-up game. When there aren't enough players to have a regular game on a *sandlot,* sides are chosen and a game is played informally.

On deck. The batter who follows the hitter at the plate. The on-deck man stands or kneels in a circle outside the dugout approximately 40 feet from home plate.

Open base. A base not occupied by a runner. Frequently, if men are on base with no or one out, but first base remains open, the pitcher will walk a batter intentionally to set up a force-out or a double play.

Opener. The first game of the season for any team; or the first game in a set or series; or the first of a doubleheader.

Opposite field. That side of the field which a batter hits to that is the same as the side he swings from. For example, a right-handed batter is hitting to the opposite field when he hits the ball to right field; or a left-handed swinger hits to left. So called because most hitters tend to *pull* the ball—that is, right-handed batters tend to hit to the left side, and vice versa.

Option. (1) Term used when a player's contract expires and he has the choice of renewing his contract or signing with another club. (2) A Major League team may send a player to the minors a certain number of times befor placing him on *waivers* and allowing any team to buy him.

Option clause. The section in some players' contracts that gives the team the right to retain a player after his contract has expired so that they can play him during the period of renegotiation.

Order. Short for batting order; the *lineup.*

Origin. Historians do not completely agree on an exact date for the first baseball game, although most contend that in 1839 in Cooperstown, New York, our national sport had its birth.

Outfield. The area within the 90-degree angle formed by the foul lines beyond the infield surface. In the Majors, the minimum distances from home plate are 325 feet to the right and left field walls, and 400 feet to dead center. The term may also refer to any player who plays right, center, or left field.

Outright. Term for a legal transaction between two teams whereby a player is sent from one club to the other solely for cash.

Outside. Refers to a pitch out of the strike zone on the side of the plate opposite the batter.

Outside baseball. Refers to an offensive strategy depending largely on power hitting rather than on good base-running, usually because the team lacks good team speed.

Outside pivot. A defensive maneuver in which the shortstop brushes the bag on the outfield side of second base prior to his relay to first on a double or triple play.

Outslug. To defeat an opposing team in a high-scoring game; or to get more hits than the opposition.

Overhand pitch (throw). A throwing motion by a pitcher (or fielder) that is executed with the arm extended straight over the shoulder. In pitching, it is the most common style of delivery.

Overmanage. Pertaining to a team's manager, to employ an excessive amount of strategy in a game to the detriment of his team. For example, if a manager signals for a hit-and-run when a poor hitter is up and a slow runner is on base, he takes the chance of giving up an easy out. Or, if he changes pitchers every time a couple of hits are surrendered, the several relievers may do worse than one or two pitchers.

Overrun. (1) To touch a base but slide or run beyond it; the player who overruns in this way can be tagged out. (2) To misjudge a batted ball by running across its path; the ball lands behind the fielder.

Overslide. To slide beyond second or third base, or first on an attempted pickoff. The runner does so accidentally and must scramble back to the base before he is tagged out.

Overstriding. Refers to a batter who takes too long a step toward the pitcher when swinging the bat. This results in frequent strikeouts and pop-ups.

Overthrow. A throw that eludes a fielder usually because it is over his head or wide to one side. It travels out of play, in the dugout or stands for example, and each runner is awarded the base he was advancing toward, plus one more.

Palm ball. A type of pitch in which the pitcher's hand completely envelops the ball, which is then thrown with a pushing motion. The ball spins very little and may "move" because of increased resistance to the air.

Pass. A *walk*. Four *balls* are thrown to a batter and he is awarded first base. (Sometimes called a free pass, free ticket to first, etc.)

Passed ball. A catcher's "error," when the official scorer thinks that the catcher should have caught a pitch that gets by him, allowing a runner to advance one base. If this occurs on the third strike, the batter may run to first; and if he reaches the base safely no out will be recorded, although the pitcher is still credited with a strikeout.

Passing a runner. Running ahead of a fellow teammate who is already running on the base paths; the player who so passes another runner is called out.

Peg. A throw made by a fielder or the catcher to the base to which a runner is advancing or trying to steal. The term is especially appropriate if the throw is accurate.

Pennant. (1) A flag with the team's name printed on it. (2) A flag symbolizing victory in a championship. (3) The championship itself within the league: in the Majors, the winners of the National and American League pennants meet each other in the World Series.

Pepper. A hitting and fielding exercise where a batter taps grounders to several fielders who stand only a short distance away; the rapidity of the action in a "game" of pepper tests the fielders' reflexes and quickness of maneuverability. Each player takes a turn hitting.

Percentage. (1) The manager's indication of the likelihood that a time-worn strategy will work; as in "playing the percentages." (2) The mathematical system used in computing averages, such as the batting, slugging, won-lost (for team or pitcher), earned run, or fielding average.

Perfect game. A most extraordinary accomplishment in which one pitcher throws a no-hit, no-walk, errorless game and all 27 batters on the opposing team are retired in order over 9 innings.

"Phenom." Derived from the word "phenomenal," a young player with exceptional ability discovered at a tryout.

Pick it. An expression referring to a player's ability to field adeptly and with consistency.

Pickle. May refer to any *rundown,* but it usually means a game played by youngsters. Players with gloves stand at each of two bases and throw the ball back and forth. One runner runs back and forth until he is tagged out.

Pickoff. A defensive play in which the catcher or pitcher throws the ball to a base from which a runner is taking his *lead* and a baseman tags the runner out. Signals between pitcher, catcher, and infielders are often used to set up the play.

Piece of the ball. A foul ball; slight rather than full contact with a pitched ball. A batter who is not hitting well is content just to try to get a piece of the ball; and a batter with 2 strikes on him wants at least to foul the ball to keep from striking out.

Pilot. The manager of a team; so called because he is at the controls, calling the shots and determining who will play.

Pinch hitter. A player who is called off the bench by the manager and assigned to bat for another player already in the lineup; that player is automatically out of the game, while the pinch hitter may or may not be assigned by the manager to fill a position on the field and bat again when his turn in the lineup comes around.

Pinch runner. A player, usually one with superior speed or outstanding base-running abilities, who comes off the bench to replace a runner already on base. Like the pinch hitter, the pinch runner himself may remain in the game at the manager's discretion.

Pitch. (1) The ball thrown by the pitcher, initiating a play. (2) To throw the ball from the mound: after his *windup,* the pitcher *delivers* the ball to the plate. Depending on his grip and wrist motion, he may be throwing a fastball, curve, slider, knuckler, screwball, change of pace, or some other pitch.

Pitch around. When a dangerous hitter comes up, the pitcher may try to throw only near or around the corners of the plate, willingly risking a walk rather than taking the chance of surrendering a *hit,* especially a long ball. This type of defensive strategy occurs most often when first base is open.

Pitcher. The hurler on the mound who throws to each batter, employing the *windup,* sometimes the *stretch* (with men on base), and the *delivery.* He must stand on the *rubber* and he may throw many different types of pitches. According to his performance in relation to the entire game action, a pitcher is officially recorded as being either the winning or the losing pitcher of the game; but only one pitcher for each team can be the *pitcher of record* for a given game. A pitcher's performance is most commonly measured in terms of his *won-lost percentage* and *earned run average.*

Pitcher covering first. A standard defensive play. On any ball hit to the right side of the infield, the first baseman may have to range to his right and be unable to get to the bag before the hitter. This situation requires that the pitcher cover first base to receive the put-out throw from the player who fields the ball.

Pitcher's elbow. An ailment caused by arm strain affecting the tendons, muscles, or nerves; may necessitate surgery or constant treatment by a trainer.

Pitchers of record. During the game, the pitchers on opposite teams who will be credited with a win or a loss if the score is not reversed; after the game, the winner and loser.

Pitching chart. An extensive record of a game that is maintained by a pitcher's teammate or friend. Every pitch is recorded, including type, ball or strike, high or low, and the result (e.g., put-out or hit, and location of hit). The pitcher studies the record to look for flaws in his technique.

Pitching duel. (1) A low-scoring game. The outcome may depend on which pitcher surrenders a single run. (2) A contest between two pitchers, usually youngsters. They throw without a batter, but someone still calls balls and strikes. The winner is the one who throws the fewest walks.

Pitching machine. Called "iron mike," it automatically sends baseballs toward home plate for the purpose of batting practice; speed is adjustable.

Pitchout. Used with a runner on base, a defensive tactic whereby the catcher signals for a pitch a foot or so *outside* when he anticipates a steal or wants to make a pickoff; he can then make a quick, unobstructed throw since the batter is unable to reach the ball.

Pivot. (1) A player's rotation on one foot when fielding and throwing the ball, or the pitcher's turning his foot on the rubber when pushing off of it. (2) The series of movements made by a second baseman or a shortstop while making a put-out at second base in the course of a double or triple play.

Platooned. Refers to two or more players who are used alternately as starters, usually when one bats opposite the other. They play the same position although generally neither one is outstanding.

Play ball! The familiar cry of the umpire to begin a game, or to resume action in the course of a game.

Playable. Describes any ball that is not "dead," especially a pop foul or a fair ball that bounces on the foul side of the line after it passes first or third base.

Player representative. A member of each Major League team who is selected for the Players' Association, an organization that engages in collective bargaining.

Player-coach. An individual who fulfills both capacities, although he usually puts greater emphasis on coaching and plays only when necessary.

Playoff. (1) A best-of-five series played between the winners of the two divisions, East and West, of both *leagues,* the National and American; the winners of the divisional playoffs win the *pennant* for their respective leagues and then play one another in the *World Series.* (2) Any game(s) played for a championship.

Pocket. The central section of the inside of the glove where most balls are caught.

Pole. (1) The foul pole which extends above the playing surface beyond the right and left field foul lines. (2) To hit the ball hard.

Pop-up. A short fly ball which is usually easy to catch for any fielder.

Pop-up slide. An offensive tactic in which the runner slides and then straightens up to his feet in one single motion, usually when he thinks he may have the opportunity to advance to another base.

Portsider. Another word for a southpaw, or left-handed pitcher.

Postponement. A game delayed by inclement weather or technical difficulties may be resumed on the same day or rescheduled for a later date. Major League games are never actually cancelled (except, on occasion, late in the season, once the pennant has been clinched, and unplayed game(s) could have no effect on the final standings).

Powerhouse. (1) A hitter known for his ability to hit the long ball. (2) A team with many power hitters.

President. An executive of either league whose duties include hiring and scheduling umpires, scheduling games, and approving contracts.

Proper cut. A batter's swing on an even or slightly downward level, aiming to hit the ball on its upper half, generally resulting in a grounder or a line drive.

Protecting the plate. (1) For batters, moving a little closer to the plate and swinging at any pitch that even looks like a strike when the batter has 2 strikes against him. (2) For catchers, guarding or obstructing home plate in anticipation of a close play with a base runner who is attempting to score.

Protecting the runner. An offensive tactic in which the batter swings and misses intentionally in order to try to distract the catcher when a runner attempts to steal.

Protective screen. Fencing or wire mesh used for protection of the pitcher and sometimes the first baseman (when he is receiving throws on grounders to infielders) during batting practice.

Protectors. Small steel pads that protect the toes, worn generally by umpires.

Protest. If either team's manager thinks that the umpire has failed to follow the rules, he must notify the umpire of his opinion before another pitch is thrown. The umpire then notifies the other manager that the game is under protest. If the claimant is correct and his team loses, the game must be played over as determined by the *commissioner*.

Pull hitter. A batter who characteristically hits the ball to the side of the field where he has the greatest strength. A right-handed hitter hits the ball to left field and a left-handed hitter hits to right. See also *Opposite field.*

Pulled hamstring. A common injury which involves strain of the tendons behind the knee that insert into thigh muscle.

Pulling the string. Expression for a pitcher's strategy of throwing a *change of pace*—a slow ball after a fast one or vice versa—to try to fool the hitter and catch him off balance.

Pump. The movement of the pitcher during his *windup* when he swings his arms back, brings them together in front, and then lifts them over his head.

Pump system. The catcher's signal for a pitch depends on how many times he flashes—pumps—his signs, rather than on how many fingers are shown.

Purchase. A legal transaction which transfers one or more players from one team to another in exchange for cash.

Push. (1) To hit the ball to the *opposite field*. (2) The pitcher's forward thrust with his foot on the rubber just prior to his delivery.

Push bunt. A swinging *bunt* where the batter taps the ball slightly harder than usual to try to get the ball past the pitcher and yet place the ball shallow in the infield.

Put-out. Defense: the opposite of getting on base. A batter strikes out, grounds or flies out, is caught "napping," stealing, or trying to advance; is forced out, or fails to "tag up" or misses a bag, etc. Three put-outs constitute one half of an inning and retire the side.

Quail shot. A weak fly ball that drips into the shallow outfield for a *hit*.

Quarterback drill. An exercise by which pitchers, and other players occasionally, practice catching the ball over their right and left shoulders to sharpen their reflexes.

Question mark. A player who may not be able to perform on a given day because of an injury.

Quick pitch. An *illegal pitch*: as soon as the ball is returned by the catcher to the pitcher, a pitch is made before the batter has time to react.

Rattle. To distract. For example, a batter rattles the pitcher by changing his stance, moving close to the plate, feigning a bunt position, and so on.

Reading. Observing a pitcher's movements so closely that a batter can detect what type pitch will be thrown as soon as the pitcher winds up.

Record. The won-lost totals for a manager, team, or pitcher. Any mathematical figure representing the achievements of a player for a game, season, or career.

Relay. A standard defensive maneuver: a fielder receives a throw from another fielder and in turn throws—relays—to a base to which a runner is advancing; especially important in double plays and in throws coming in from the outfield.

Release. (1) A player is cut from the team and/or sent to the Minors. (2) Said of a ball that leaves the pitcher's or any fielder's hand.

Reliever (relief pitcher). A pitcher who comes in the game to substitute for a starter or another relief pitcher. The staff of relievers, who remain in the *bullpen*, usually comprises five or six such pitchers.

Replacement. A substitute. When he enters the game, whether to bat, run, or to take the field or the mound, the player he replaces must leave the game.

Right fielder. The outfielder positioned near the right foul line. His duties include fielding balls to either side and in front of and behind him, as well as making throws to the bases.

Right-center. The area of the outfield between the right and center fielders where many gap shots travel.

Rookie. A first year player.

Rosin. Resin sewn into a bag that comes readily through the material in the form of powder. Pitchers and batters use it on their hands to get a better grip.

Roster. The players who constitute a team, usually limited to a specific number. In the Majors, only 25 active players suit up from a month after the season to September 1.

Rotation. Refers to the cycle of participation among pitchers. Most Major League teams use 4 starting pitchers, and each one starts every fourth game. The remaining five or six pitchers on the staff are used for *relief*.

Roundhouse. A *curve ball* with a wide arc that comes sweeping across the plate.

Rounding a base. When a runner approaches a base, he swerves to the right side of the base path so that he can minimize the distance he has to travel to the next base. When rounding the bases, runners are allowed to swerve 15 feet beyond the base line.

Rubber. A slab measuring 24 inches by 6 inches imbedded in the dirt atop the pitcher's *mound* no more than 10 inches above the field. It is located 60 feet 6 inches from home plate in line with second base. The pitcher must begin his delivery with one foot on the rubber.

Rubber arm. An expression referring to a pitcher who has an arm that seems impervious to injury or fatigue.

Rubber band. A derogatory expression describing a pitcher who has a weak or weary arm.

Rubber-coated baseball. A ball specially designed for indoor use. In the winter, many players work out with them in gymnasiums during the off-season.

Run. A score made when a runner safely crosses home plate.

This may occur in a number of ways, including a home run, a run batted in on a hit, walk, or sacrifice, or a runner scoring from third on a squeeze, walk, or passed ball.

Run batted in (RBI). A run produced by a *hit, walk,* or *sacrifice.* The RBI king is the player in the league with the highest total by the season's end.

Run-and-hit. An offensive play in which the runner breaks toward the next base and the batter hits the ball if he chooses. The batter's choice differentiates this play from the *hit-and-run.*

Rundown. A situation in which a runner is caught between two bases and is pursued by fielders who throw the ball back and forth until a tag can be made.

Sack. A base, especially the three besides home plate that are made of canvas.

Sacrifice. An offensive play in which the batter is out, usually on a bunt or a fly ball to the outfield, but a runner advances. If the runner scores, the batter still gets credit for a *run batted in (RBI).*

Safe. The ruling conferred upon any runner who reaches base without being put out, forced out, or tagged.

Sandlot. An empty lot or a dirt clearing used for pick-up games, usually by youngsters.

Save. An accomplishment of a relief pitcher who enters the game with his team ahead and pitches a minimum of three innings to preserve a victory for the pitcher of record.

Sawed-off bat. A bat shaved smooth at the top to reduce air friction on the swing; primarily for a batter who requires greater thrust because of a small upper torso.

Scatter arm. A pitcher or fielder who throws with a lack of consistency, often resulting in costly errors.

Scattered. Refers to a few *hits* spread out over many innings, resulting in few or no runs.

Schedule. Each Major League team plays 162 games, half at home and half away. They usually play three or four consecutive games with a team before playing another club. Scheduling is the responsibility of the league President.

Science. The entire canon of strategy and technique employed by coaches and players alike. Experts disagree on whether baseball is primarily a sport depending on instinct and inborn ability, or scientifically acquired skills that may be learned by anyone. Probably, it involves a fusion of the two.

Score. To tally a *run,* whether it is *earned* or *unearned.* The object of baseball is to accumulate more runs than the opposition.

Scoreboard. A large structure beyond and above the outfield where the lineups, the score, the count, the number of outs, etc., are electronically recorded. It is also sometimes used for comic illustrations of the game's events.

Scorecard. A sheet on which every play in a game is recorded. Players are listed in their batting order and spaces are provided for marking the result of each time at bat. The card can be used to compute various statistical data such as strikeouts, walks, and errors. On put-outs, the scorer indicates the fielder(s) who made the play with numbers corresponding to each position: pitcher-1; catcher-2; first baseman-3; second baseman-4; third baseman-5; shortstop-6; left fielder-7; center fielder-8; right fielder-9.

Scoring position. A runner on second or third base may score on almost any hit to the outfield. If a pitcher leaves the game, he is responsible for all runners in such position, as well as a runner on first.

Scout. A member of a baseball club (who may also be a coach or fulfill some other position) who travels about looking for new talent. He views minor, semiprofessional, college, and high school leagues, etc.

Screen. (1) The fencing or wire mesh used to protect the pitcher and first baseman during batting practice; or the mesh behind home plate which prevents foul balls from injuring the spectators. (2) A runner between the fielder and the ball; he cannot touch the ball or the fielder.

Screwball. A pitch that moves in toward the batter—unlike the *curve,* which moves away from him. The pitcher twists his wrist inward rather than outward as he throws.

Scribe. A sports writer.

Scrimmage. A practice session resembling an inner-squad game except that the defense remains in the field and batters take turns hitting and running no matter how many put-outs are made.

Scrub. A derogatory term for a substitute or a player who lacks natural ability.

Season. The period from April to October when all regular games are scheduled. Major League teams play 162 games, preceded by several months training, and followed by playoffs and the World Series for the victors.

Second baseman. The infielder normally positioned on the right side of the diamond between first and second base. His duties include covering first on a bunt, covering second on a steal or a double play, and relaying throws in from the outfield.

Seeing-eye. A *hit* that barely eludes two defenders as if it had eyes of its own.

Set. (1) The point in a pitcher's *windup* when both arms come down to about waist level, prior to the kick of the leg. (2) A short series of games played against the same team.

Set tag. A defensive maneuver in which a fielder puts his glove containing the ball on the ground immediately in front of the bag and waits for a runner to slide into it, making a put-out.

Seventh-inning stretch. The traditional pause before the seventh inning, when the spectators stand and exercise their stiff bodies or go to the concessions for refreshments.

Shagging. Catching fly balls and retrieving hits during batting practice.

Shake-off. A gesture by which the pitcher rejects the catcher's signal and requests another one, usually by waving his glove.

Shallow. Refers to any ball hit in the area of the outfield close to the infield diamond.

Shave. A high and hard *brush-back* pitch that just misses the batter's face or head.

Shell. To hit a pitcher very well and to score many runs in the process.

Shift. (1) A defensive strategy whereby infielders or outfielders move markedly to one side of the field to compensate for a particular hitter. For example, the second baseman moves to the left field side of second base for a right-handed *pull* hitter. (2) Players may switch positions during the course of the game.

Shin guard. A durable piece of moulded or plastic equipment strapped to the lower leg of the catcher and home plate umpire to prevent injury, especially on pitches in the dirt and foul tips.

Shoestring catch. The fielder catches the ball at his shoe tops or just above the ground after running at top speed and making a stab or dive.

Short fielder. The tenth man in slow-pitch *softball* who is usually positioned somewhere in the shallow outfield.

Short hop. A very low bounce that skips off the field surface into a fielder's glove on a hit or a low throw.

Short man. On a relay coming in from the outfield, the infielder who backs up the *cut-off* man in case of an overthrow by the outfielder.

Short relief. Refers to a reliever coming in and pitching toward the end of a game. To get a *save,* he must pitch at least 3 innings.

Short-arm. A throw made with the arm close to or across the body, without full extension. The fielder is usually off-balance or only a short distance from another fielder receiving the throw.

Shortstop. The infielder normally positioned on the left side of the diamond between second and third base. His duties include covering second on a steal or a double play, covering third on a bunt when there are runners on first and second, relaying throws in from the outfield, and making plays *in the hole*.

Shotgun. A player, particularly an outfielder, who has a very strong arm. Some can throw the ball on a fly from the wall or fence to home plate.

Shovel. To throw the ball weakly in an underhand motion when off-balance or when very close to the fielder receiving the throw.

Shutout. A victory in which one or more pitchers on a team manage to hold the opposition scoreless in an entire game.

Sidearm. A throwing motion with the arm extended outward from the hip or side rather than straight over the shoulder. When the pitcher uses this motion, the ball comes in on an angle and may be difficult for the batter to pick up.

Sign. (1) A signal. (2) The catcher conceals his fingers from the batter by putting them between his legs. The number of fingers or the number of times they are "flashed" determines what type pitch will be thrown. With a runner on second who can see the catcher, possibly "steal" his signal, and relay a message to the batter, the catcher usually changes his sign.

Signal. (1) A catcher's sign. (2) Gestures made by fielders, batters, or coaches to communicate messages to one or more members of the same team without being detected by the opposition. For example, the third base coach tips his hat to indicate a hit-and-run; the runner knows to break toward the next base, and the batter knows that he must try to hit the ball.

Silver Glove Award. Presented annually to Minor League players who have the highest fielding *averages* at their respective positions; eight such awards are given.

Single. A one-base *hit*. The batter reaches first base safely after hitting the ball in fair territory without an error being committed by a fielder.

Singleton. A single run scored in any inning.

Sinker. A pitch thrown with the standard grip except that the index and middle fingertips are raised above the ball, causing the pitch to drop in front of the plate.

Sitting duck. A base runner who tries to steal or advance and is out by a wide margin. This often occurs when the catcher calls for a *pitchout* on a steal.

Sizzler. A good hard fastball.

Skipper. The *manager* of the team. His duties include determining the roster, making the lineup for each game, and directing the strategy used in a game.

Skyscraper. A high fly ball straight up into the air that is pursued by the catcher between home plate and the stands. This is one of the *catcher's* most common and difficult plays.

Slash bunt. See *Bunt*.

Slide. An offensive maneuver in which the runner's feet leave the ground as he approaches a base; he may try to catch one corner of the bag with his foot or hand as he lands. Some runners prefer to go head first with a dive, thereby freeing their hands to possibly elude the fielder's tag.

Slider. A pitch thrown with an outward twist of the wrist like the *curve* and with velocity only slightly less than a *fastball*; designed to curve slightly away from the batter.

Sliding tomato. A baseball, especially when it is pitched.

Slip pitch. A pitch thrown like a *palm ball* except that the fingertips are raised above the ball's surface; this results in decreased forward momentum, causing a sudden drop in trajectory near the plate.

Slugfest. A high-scoring game in which both teams accumulate many *hits*.

Slugger. A powerful batter who hits consistently for long distance.

Slugging percentage. A variation of the *batting average* obtained by dividing the total number of bases reached on safe *hits*, by the number of official *at-bats,* to the nearest thousandth. For example, a batter with 6 total bases in 10 at-bats averages .600.

Slump. An extended period of time during which a team or an individual player performs far below potential. Poor pitching, hitting, or fielding may be involved.

Smash. A very hard hit ball, especially if it is hit for a long distance.

Smoke. An expression used to describe the effect of a good hard *fastball,* which may reach a velocity close to 100 mph.

Softball. An offshoot of baseball, played in a similar manner with a few exceptions. Bases are 60 feet apart and pitchers throw fast or slow, depending on the particular league. In slow-pitch, there are 10 players, including a short-fielder who usually plays somewhere in the shallow outfield. A hit batsman does not get a free ticket to first as he would in fast pitch. There are 9 players in fast pitch; runners can steal after the pitch passes the batter.

Southpaw. A left-handed thrower, especially a pitcher.

Spear. To catch a sharply hit ball, especially if it is to one side of the fielder or up above his head.

Spectator's interference. When in the judgment of the umpire a fan prevents a fielder from making a play, the batter is called out and the fan may be ejected from the stadium.

Spiked. Refers to a painful cut or bruise sustained most often by a fielder making a tag on a runner, or relaying a throw on a double or a triple play when the runner tries to break up the play.

Spikes. Shoes with metal, plastic, or rubber projections on the bottom worn by players to increase traction. The word derives from the era when only metal-cleated shoes were worn, but now "cleats" and "spikes" are used interchangeably.

Spin his cap. To throw a *beanball* or a *brush-back* pitch high and inside to intimidate the batter.

Spitball. An illegal pitch. The pitcher places a foreign substance on the ball, usually saliva, giving the pitch the name "spitter." The pitch drops suddenly because of the imbalance of weight on the ball.

Splinters. A derogatory exaggeration for what substitutes get in their pants as a result of sitting on the bench.

Split. An equal division of victory and loss: each opposing team wins an equal number of games in a *set* or a *doubleheader.*

Spoiler. A team or player who defeats an opponent who is pursuing an important victory. For example, a batter gets a hit off a pitcher who had a no-hitter going; or a team beats an opponent that is in contention for the playoffs.

Spot starter. A pitcher who is not in the normal *rotation* but who occasionally starts when he is needed.

Spray hitter. A batter who hits the ball to all fields with generally the same proficiency; usually a characteristic of a hitter who has a high *average.*

Spring training. The period of preseason workouts when players are conditioned and drilled in baseball technique. Minor leaguers and others are given tryouts and selections are made for the team roster. Exhibition games are played with other clubs for practice.

Squeaker. A very close game whose outcome is usually decided by a single run.

Squeeze play. An offensive play in which a runner on third base begins to advance toward home during the pitcher's wind-up, and the batter tries to bunt the ball; also called a suicide squeeze.

Stance. The manner in which a batter stands at the plate. In the conventional or "open" stance, the left foot is several inches closer to the plate than the right. In the "closed" stance, the position of the feet is reversed.

Standings. The teams in each division are listed in the order of their won-lost percentage, including the number of *games* a team is behind the first place team.

Stand-up. Applies to a batter who gets a double, triple, or inside-the-park home run without having to slide.

Starting rotation. Pitchers on the staff who receive starting assignments regularly. In the Majors, each team usually employs four starters, each of whom pitches every fourth game.

Steal. The runner's attempt to advance a base by running on or immediately after the pitch rather than on a hit, passed ball, wild pitch, etc. The runner steals on the pitcher when he gets a good *jump*; he steals on the catcher when he takes advantage of a weak or inaccurate throw. The runner breaks while the pitcher is winding up, unless it is a *delayed* steal.

Stealing signals. Observing the opposing coaches or catcher to see what strategy is employed after a particular sign is given in order to learn the signs and be able to predict the opposition's movements. Some clubs have been known to use binoculars to steal the catcher's signs. When a runner is on second, he has a clear view of the catcher and so a different set of signals may be used. Many managers change their code from game to game.

Stepping on the plate. If the batter does so while swinging or beginning to run, he is called out.

Stepping out of the box. If the batter does so before the pitcher's windup, a time-out is called. If he does so during the windup, the pitcher can deliver the ball and it is an official pitch.

Sting. (1) To hit the ball sharply. (2) A sensation in the hands and arms that is the frequent result of hitting on a cold day.

Stopper. A consistent pitcher who can be counted on in the *clutch* to win a crucial game—like snapping a losing streak or winning a game to get his team into the playoffs. This term also refers to a good relief pitcher who can come in and keep the opposition from scoring.

Straddle pivot. A defensive maneuver in which the second baseman stands with his feet on either side of the bag and drags his foot across the base after he receives a throw from a fielder on a double or triple play; he then makes his relay to first.

Straightaway. Refers to the outfielders who assume their normal positions for a batter who hits to all fields.

Stranded. Refers to runners who are *left on base* (LOB) at the end of an inning.

Strawberry. An abrasion or brushburn which usually results from a slide or dive because of friction with the playing surface.

Streak. An uninterrupted accumulation of victories, losses, errorless games, games in which a batter gets at least one hit, or some other repetitive achievement.

Stretch. (1) A pitcher's stance on the mound: when one or more bases are occupied, the pitcher winds up with his foot parallel to the rubber and he pauses—makes the stretch—when he comes to the *set* position to try to keep the runners from taking too long a lead. (2) Applies also to the first baseman: while keeping one foot on the bag, the first baseman extends his opposite foot forward and reaches out with his arm as far as he can for a fielder's throw to try to get the ball before the batter crosses the bag.

Stretching a hit. An aggressive runner advances one or more bases beyond where most batters would stop. For example, on a hit to right field that would normally be a single, the batter runs hard and makes it to second.

Strike. Any pitch in the strike zone not hit in fair territory by the batter; any pitch swung on and missed by the batter; a foul ball with less than 2 strikes on the batter not caught on the fly by a fielder; a foul tip caught by the catcher with 2 strikes on the batter. Three strikes are a put-out and the pitcher is credited with a strikeout.

Strike zone. The rectangular area formed by the batter's knees and armpits vertically and the width of the plate horizontally, within which area the pitcher tries to throw a strike. (See Appendix, p. 92.)

Strikeout (SO *or* **K).** An out made when the pitcher throws 3 strikes to a batter and the catcher holds on to the final pitch. On a *passed ball,* the runner may advance to first; if he does, no put-out is recorded, although the pitcher is still credited with a strikeout.

Stroke. A nice even swing, usually resulting in a line drive to the outfield.

Study. For a batter to observe a pitcher closely, or a pitcher to observe a batter, in order to learn the habits or techniques of one's adversary.

Stuff. Refers in general to the arsenal of pitches used by a particular pitcher, especially when he is effective. These may include the fastball, slider, curve, knuckler, changeup, screwball, etc.

Submarine. A throw or a pitch delivered with an underhand motion; it may nevertheless reach a high velocity.

Substitute. A player who replaces a teammate in the lineup, unless it is the pitcher. The player who is replaced may not return to the game.

Substitute runner. A player sent into the game when speed on the base paths is particularly important. The player who is replaced may not return to the game; the substitute may remain in the game at the manager's discretion.

Suicide squeeze. See *Squeeze play.*

Suspended game. One that will be completed at a later date because of a legal curfew, darkness, or because the game has exceeded the time limits established by the league.

Sweep. Consecutive victories in a *set* or series of games without sustaining a loss.

Sweeping. A batting defect in which the batter's arms are swung too far from his body and his swing is weak and poorly controlled.

Swing. The batter holds the bat in both hands and tries to hit the ball by stepping toward the pitcher with one foot, swinging both arms, and moving his body slightly toward the plate to get greater force behing the swing.

Swing away. A directive to a batter in a situation where he would normally be signalled to *take* a pitch (e.g., 3-0 or 3-1 *count*), indicating that he is allowed to hit instead.

Swing from the heels. An expression describing the batter who puts all of his power into a swing to try to hit a long ball, often resulting in an overswing. Most batters hit better with a normal swing.

Swinging bunt. A hitting technique in which the batter swings very softly to try to hit the ball just past the pitcher.

Switch hitter. A batter who can hit either right- or left-handed. Most will bat from the right side against left-handed pitching and the opposite way against right-handed pitching.

Tag. For a fielder to touch the runner with the ball in his bare hand or in his glove. If the runner is off base, he is out.

Tagging up. Waiting until a fly ball is caught before trying to advance a base. If a runner tags and goes from third to home, the batter is credited with a *sacrifice* and a *run batted in.*

Tail away. An expression which refers to any pitch that moves down and away from a batter, or a hit that veers away from a fielder.

Take. The opposite of to swing. The batter doesn't swing because either he chooses not to or the coach signals him. Some hitters "take" until a strike is thrown; almost all do so when the count is 3-0.

"Take him over the wall." A familiar exhortation from players or fans to a batter to encourage him to hit a home run.

Tally. To score a run, whether it is *earned* or *unearned.* The object of the game is to tally more runs than the opposition.

Tape measure. Refers to a long home run or the estimated distance that the ball travels.

Tar. Like *rosin;* players rub this on their bat to get a better grip.

Target. The catcher's mitt is where the pitcher tries to throw; it may be moved in and out or up and down within the *strike zone.*

Team. All of the players who are under contract with a team, whether or not they are on the active *roster;* occasionally, additional players are kept for emergency use.

Team meeting. An assembly of the team called by a player or coach to discuss an important matter—like why the team is losing—or to resolve problems of morale or dissention.

Tear. A hot streak for a team when they win many games; or for a player when he hits exceptionally well.

Tee. An adjustable mechanism on top of which a baseball is placed. Amateur players hit the ball from the tee to practice their swing.

Tee off. To take a very full cut when trying for a home run against an especially weak pitcher.

Telegraph. By using very characteristic mannerisms or movements, a pitcher gives away—telegraphs—his pitch to the batter. For example, if he always throws his curve with a sidearm motion and never throws any other pitch with that delivery, the batter will know when the curve is coming.

Territory. The general area which any fielder is responsible for covering. For example, the right fielder should ideally be able to get any ball between him and the stands on the right side, any hit over his head or in the gap between him and the center fielder, and any shallow hit beyond the reach of the infielders on the right side of the diamond.

Texas leaguer. A weakly hit fly ball that drops in the *shallow* outfield for a hit.

Third base coach. He fulfills a role similar to that of the first base coach, except that he decides whether a runner will stop at third or advance to home. He usually also gives signals to the batter.

Third baseman. The infielder positioned on the left side of the diamond near third base, an area called "the hot corner." His duties include fielding bunts, knocking down balls hit down the line, and receiving throws from the outfield.

Third strike dropped. When the catcher does this, the batter is not out if he can beat the catcher's throw to first base, although the pitcher is still credited with a strikeout.

Threat. A team that is so good that it will almost certainly be in contention for the pennant; or a player whose expertise in one or more facets of the game is so well known that he is feared by the opposition, e.g., in stealing or hitting the long ball.

Three-bagger. A *triple;* any hit where the batter reaches third base safely without an error being committed by a fielder.

Three-hundred hitter. A batter with an *average* of .300 or above is considered very good and usually hits near the top of the lineup.

Three-quarters delivery. A pitching style in which the pitcher's arm is extended at about a 45-degree angle, about halfway between *overhand* and *sidearm,* when he makes his delivery to the plate.

Throw out. A defensive play in which a fielder throws to a base to which a runner is advancing and gets him out on a force or a tag.

Throwing darts. Pitching with excellent control, especially when a pitcher can hit the *target* on almost every pitch.

Tie. A game that ends without either team victorious. Whether or not extra innings have been played, the game must be rescheduled for a later date in the Major Leagues.

Time out. A temporary pause in the game called by the umpire; a player may request him to do so.

Timing. One of the most important aspects of hitting. The batter must be able to gauge when the ball is at the proper distance from the plate to begin his swing. When he can do so regularly, he will probably hit solidly and consistently.

To the shower. An expression referring to the place where the pitcher may douse himself after being relieved by another pitcher.

Top. (1) Of the *inning:* the time when the visiting team bats, consisting of 3 put-outs. (2) Of the *order:* the first few hitters in the lineup, who are usually the most consistent and the most powerful.

Total bases (TB). The total reached safely by a team or an individual player, including advances made on sacrifices and steals. The total number that a batter gets on each hit is used to compute his *slugging percentage.*

Trade. A legal transaction which transfers one or more players from one team to another in exchange for another player or players. Cash may or may not be involved. In the Majors, deals can be made during the season until June 15.

Trade bait. Whenever a team can afford to trade a player or must trade to fill a gap, the general manager selects certain players to be offered in negotiations. An old player who has only a few years left, or a good player who may attract good offers from other teams, is considered good bait.

Trading block. When a player becomes good *trade bait* or plays so poorly that he becomes expendable to a team, the general manager makes it known to other teams that he is interested in trading the player.

Trainer. Most clubs have two such employees who oversee the players' conditioning with weight training, massage, calisthenics, etc.; like a physician, they also administer treatment for injuries.

Trap. A runner caught off base by a quick throw from an alert player, usually the catcher.

Trapped ball. A *hit* that results when a fielder catches the ball that comes in contact with another surface such as the field or the wall, thereby nullifying the catch.

Triple. A three-base *hit*. The batter reaches third base safely after hitting the ball in fair territory and no error is committed by a fielder.

Triple crown. A most unusual and spectacular feat, when a player manages to win the *batting, home run,* and *runs batted in* titles all in one year.

Triple play. A rare occurrence whenever 3 offensive players are out on the same play. The batter is usually one of these, although the manner of executing the play may differ. For example, a line drive that looks like a hit is caught and 2 runners are caught off base; the bases are tagged by fielders who receive throws before the runner can return. Or, with first and second occupied, the third baseman catches a grounder, steps on third, throws to second, and the second baseman throws to first in time for the third out.

Tryout. An amateur player is given a chance to demonstrate his skills and ability on the field of a Major League team which may be interested in signing him to a contract.

Tunneler. A player who assumes a false role of authority by giving directives like a manager.

Turn the ball over. To throw *overhand* on a pitch, especially with the screwball when the overhand delivery is critical.

Tweener. A ball hit in the outfield that barely eludes two defenders; a *seeing-eye.*

Twenty-game winner. A pitcher who wins 20 games in a season (especially if he doesn't lose very many) is considered exceptional by Major League standards.

Twin bill. A doubleheader.

Two-bagger. A double, or two-base *hit*: any hit where the batter reaches second base safely without an error being committed by a fielder.

Umpire. The referee or arbiter in a blue uniform who enforces the rules of the game. The home plate umpire wears protective equipment similar to the catcher's and he and the other umpires wear blue caps with very small bills. The plate umpire also calls balls and strikes and rules on plays at the plate; he is the chief of the crew. Others rule on plays in the vicinity of the other three bases and in the outfield.

Umpire's interference. Occurs when the umpire either hinders a throw being made on a steal or touches a fair ball before it gets to a fielder; the play is usually taken over.

Unassisted. On a double or triple paly, one fielder makes the first or the first 2 put-outs without the aid of any other fielder, and then he makes his *relay* to first. He usually begins the play by tagging the bag for a *force-out* on the runner who is trying to advance.

Unconditional release. Pertains to a player who is trying out with a team or is unsigned for any reason. He may be let go without any obligations pending on him or the club.

Unearned run. A *run* is considered unearned whenever a score is made as a result of an error. Any subsequent runs that are scored in the inning after an unearned run—one that would otherwise have been an out—are also considered unearned.

Uniform. For any given team, outfits worn by players and coaches are generally identical in style and color. They comprise a visor cap with the team's initial or insignia on it; a short-sleeve shirt with the team's name printed on the front and the player's number on the back; a long-sleeved jersey with sleeves the same color as the uniform underneath the shirt;

pants which go just below the knees where stockings take over; and spiked shoes. Many teams have begun to wear "pajama" uniforms which have a pullover shirt and an elastic waist band on the pants.

Unsportsmanlike conduct. Behavior unbefitting a professional or amateur player or coach, including hiding the ball, fighting, distracting the opposition in an unfair way, swearing or arguing for a prolonged time with the umpire, and striking another player or the umpire. The penalty is usually ejection from the game.

Up the middle. The area around second base which is the territory of both the second baseman and the shortstop; the area where many *singles* travel.

Uppercut. An unward swing, often resulting in a fly ball, generally considered a defect in batting.

Utility man. A fielder, frequently a substitute, who can capably play several different positions.

Velocity. The speed at which a pitch travels, reaching as high as 100 mph or so on an exceptional fastball.

Verbal signals. *Signs* given by the use of key words or expressions. For example, if the coach says "base hit 'em," he may actually mean that the batter is to bunt.

Veteran. Familiarly, any player who is not a *rookie;* technically, any player who has completed eight full seasons in the major leagues.

Vine. A player's normal street clothes when he is out of uniform.

Visiting team. The team that travels from its home field to the field of an opponent. Visitors bat first, whereas the home team has the final chance to score.

Waivers. Before a player can be demoted to the Minor Leagues, or released unconditionally, he can be purchased by any team for a set amount. The last-place team has first choice, and so on up through the standings.

Walk. An offensive bonus—or a pitcher's lapse—whereby four *balls* are thrown to the batter, who is thus awarded free passage to first base. But sometimes the pitcher issues a walk intentionally: for example, when a dangerous hitter is up, first base is *open,* and there are one or more runners in scoring position. The intentional walk thus sets up the defense for a potential double play. Any walk is also commonly called a base on balls.

Warmup. (1) Limbering or throwing exercise prior to a game or practice. (2) A pitcher's throws prior to an inning or before his stint in *relief.* He is allowed a maximum of 15 of these.

Warmup jacket. A windbreaker used for warming up when the muscles are not yet loose and are more susceptible to strain. Pitchers usually don one to prevent a chilled arm, even when they reach base during the game.

Warning track. The band of dirt beyond the outfield grass that warns outfielders of the possibility of colliding into the wall or fence.

Waste pitch. A widely used pitching tactic: The pitcher throws a *ball* intentionally off target, usually when there are no balls and 2 strikes on the batter: the hitter will be most anxious to protect the plate at this time, thus incurring a strikeout risk, while at the same time the pitcher lowers his risk of surrending a *hit* to the batter.

Web. The top section of the glove opposite the fingers; made of very flexible leather for fielding balls that are difficult to reach.

Wheels. A runner's legs, especially if he's fast.

Whiff. To strike out whether by swinging or by being *caught looking.*

Whip. A *sidearm* delivery, so called because the ball comes in from either side of the mound and is usually more difficult for the batter to see.

Whitewash. To shutout a team, that is, hold it scoreless in a complete game.

Wiffle Ball®. A perforated plastic ball used by youngsters to play "baseball." They also use a plastic bat, and both items are designed for safety.

Wild. Lacking accuracy in throwing, an especially serious flaw for a pitcher. A wild pitcher will surrender many walks and *wild pitches,* such that the opposition does not even have to hit to score.

Wild pitch. A pitch thrown beyond the catcher's reach, enabling a runner to advance a base. The distinction between wild pitch and *passed ball* is often not obvious, and is left to the judgment of the *official scorer.*

Willow. A term for a baseball bat. Most bats were made of willow wood at one time, although most manufacturers have switched to ash in recent years.

Windup. The pitcher's movements prior to his *delivery.* In the standard type, he begins with the ball in his pitching hand inside his glove. He swings both arms back and then brings them together in front and raises them over his head; he turns his body to one side and raises one leg as he brings both arms down. With the foot on the rubber, he pushes off in the direction of the plate; his pitching hand comes out of his glove and his arm extends toward the plate as he releases the ball.

Winning pitcher. The hurler on the winning team who completes a game. He may pitch an incomplete game and still be the winning pitcher if his team is ahead when he is relieved. If a team is loosing when a reliever comes in and they go ahead while he is still in the game, he may become the winner.

Won-lost percentage. The team's status in the *standings* is found by dividing the number of victories by the total number of games, omitting ties, taken to the nearest thousandth. For example, with 6 wins and 3 losses, a team averages .666.

Wood man. A term for the batter, because he is wielding a wooden bat. Made most often from ash, the bat may also be made of willow and of wood from other trees.

World Series. Beginning in 1884, winners of the National League met the winners of the American Association in a series of post-season championship games. This tradition continues: the contenders from each league must win the best of 7 games for the "world's" championship.

World Series ring. An article of jewelry worn by players and coaches on the championship team; it is garnished in a manner to display the significance of such an achievement.

Wrinkle. A curve that breaks only slightly and is usually very easy for a batter to hit.

Wrist hitter. A batter who whips his wrists around to get power into his swing. Most good hitters rely more on their wrists than sheer body strength.

Wrong turn. First base is the only base which a player can legally overrun. He can even stay within fair territory after he has passed the bag. However, any motion whatsoever in the direction of second base is ruled a wrong turn, and the runner may be tagged out.

Yank a pitcher. To replace the pitcher in the game with a *reliever.* A manager may not come to the mound twice within one inning without removing the pitcher on the second trip.

Zamboni. A machine resembling a vacuum cleaner, used to suck water off of an artificial surface such as *Astroturf*.

Appendix

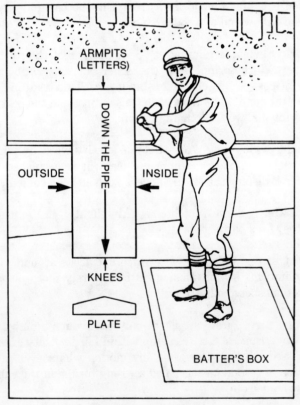

The Strike Zone

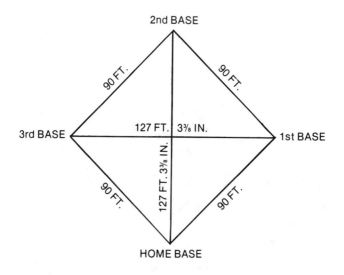

The Diamond

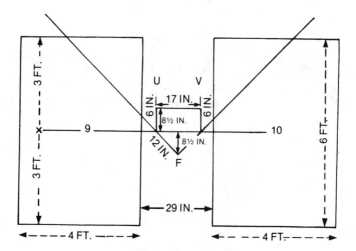

The Batter's Boxes

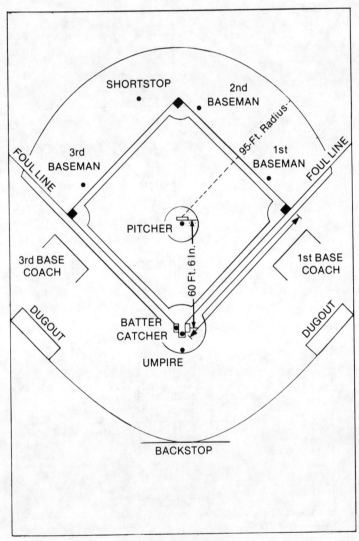

The Infield